p. 250 →

R**I**CH
WOMAN ™

A book on investing for women

Because I Hate
Being Told
What To Do!

by Kim  ki

Forewords by Robert Kiyosaki and Sharon Lechter

RICH
WOMAN™

A book on investing for women

Because I Hate
Being Told
What To Do!

by Kim Kiyosaki

Forewords by Robert Kiyosaki and Sharon Lechter

RICH
PRESS

An Imprint of Rich Publishing, LLC

Published by RICHPRESS™ An Imprint of Rich Publishing, LLC

Visit our Web sites at www.richwoman.com and www.richdad.com

Table of Contents

Foreword	BY ROBERT KIYOSAKI	1
Foreword	BY SHARON LECHTER	3
Introduction		7
Chapter One	LUNCH WITH THE GIRLS	19
Chapter Two	THE GIRLS	25
Chapter Three	MY STORY	33
Chapter Four	TWENTY YEARS AGO... IN THE ISLANDS	47
Chapter Five	IT'S ABOUT MORE THAN MONEY	53
Chapter Six	"I DON'T HAVE THE TIME"	65
Chapter Seven	WHAT DOES IT MEAN TO BE	
	FINANCIALLY INDEPENDENT?	77
Chapter Eight	"I'M NOT SMART ENOUGH"	87
Chapter Nine	HOW TO GET SMARTER QUICKLY	99
Chapter Ten	"I'M SCARED STIFF"	105
Chapter Eleven	HOW WEALTHY ARE YOU?	117
Chapter Twelve	"I DON'T HAVE THE MONEY!"	129
Chapter Thirteen	MORE ABOUT THE MONEY	141
Chapter Fourteen	"MY PARTNER'S NOT INTERESTED!"	149
Chapter Fifteen	WHY WOMEN MAKE GREAT INVESTORS	163
Chapter Sixteen	"I'M READY TO START!"	175
Chapter Seventeen	NINETY PERCENT OF SUCCESS IS	
	JUST SHOWING UP!	181
Chapter Eighteen	LET THE PROCESS BEGIN!	189
Chapter Nineteen	THREE TYPES OF MEN/	
	THREE TYPES OF INVESTMENTS	201
Chapter Twenty	THE FIRST FOUR KEYS TO	
	BEING A SUCCESSFUL INVESTOR	213
Chapter Twenty-One	THE NEXT FIVE KEYS TO	
	BEING A SUCCESSFUL INVESTOR	225
Chapter Twenty-Two	"SHOW ME THE PLAN!"	237
Chapter Twenty-Three	FULL THROTTLE!	245
Chapter Twenty Four	DINNER WITH THE GIRLS – A CELEBRATION	. . .255
A Final Thought		261
Glossary		263

Dedication

***This book is dedicated to my Mom and Dad,
Winnie and Bill Meyer.***

BY ROBERT KIYOSAKI

There is a saying that goes, "Behind every successful man is a powerful woman." In my case, this saying is definitely true. I would not have achieved the success I have, if not for my wife Kim. Sometimes I wonder where I would be if not for her.

Obviously, when I met Kim, it was her outer beauty that attracted me. On our first date, I found out she was not just a pretty face. She had a brain. She was very smart. As we got to know each other, I found out she was more beautiful on the inside than on the outside, and that is when I fell in love. If there is such a thing as soul mates, I believe I have found mine.

Yet, it was when times were tough that I found out she had a backbone. She had an inner strength that carried us through some of the toughest times I have faced and doubt I could have gotten through without her. There were many times – times when we were out of money, no roof over our head, no transportation – that she would hold me and let me just cry like a little boy. She was the brave one, the backbone, the one who never lost faith in me, although I had lost faith in myself.

As with most couples, we have had our arguments, our disagreements. We definitely do not live an Ozzie and Harriet life. Yet one of the great things about the hard times – the ups and down, the mistakes – is that what grew out of my love for Kim is respect. She is her own woman. She does not need me to take care of her. She is modern, hip, fun, rich, kind, loving, gorgeous, and independent.

When we play golf together, she tees off from the men's tees. She does not ask for nor expect a handicap just because she is a woman.

And, unfortunately, she often out-drives me and out-scores me. Thank god she does not rub it in when she wins.

When we met, all I had was a lot of debt, a ton of mistakes, great lessons in life, and a dream. She was willing to share a life with me, even though I had nothing, in order to make those dreams come true. Today, we both have gone far beyond those early dreams and currently are living dreams beyond those of our wildest imagination.

I know she did not marry me for my money, because when we met I was out of money. As to investing, all I did was teach her what my Rich Dad taught me. She took to investing like a duck to water. Today, she is a far better investor than I am, putting together deals   far bigger than I have ever done. She is a self-made woman. A Rich Woman.

That is why I am very proud to be writing this foreword for her first of many books. She is my idea of a role model for a modern woman – fun, loving, kind, beautiful, independent, smart, and rich. When it comes to money and investing she knows what she is talking about. I have seen her grow from a young woman who knew nothing about money and investing to a rich woman who is an authority on the subject. Kim practices what she preaches. It is with great pleasure that I write this foreword for my best friend, my business partner, and my wife, Kim.

BY SHARON LECHTER

Kim has been my friend and business partner for more than 10 years. I am honored that she asked me to write this foreword and welcome the opportunity to share my experience with Kim and her passion.

Many people immediately think it is easy for Kim to invest because she is Robert's wife. We hear the recurring statement, "Easy for you to say!" But being married to someone so visible and charismatic actually makes it harder to be independent and successful in one's own right. Kim has been at Robert's side and traveled the world with him educating millions of people about money and investing for more than 20 years. During that time she also focused on implementing her own investing plan and in the process built a multi-million-dollar real estate empire of her own.

I can honestly say that Kim is a fiercely independent woman, and her passion to help other women gain their financial independence is at the core of her spirit. It would have been very easy for Kim to enjoy the "good life" with the success of our company and her other investments. But instead, at a time when she has gained her own financial independence, she is now dedicating her efforts to encouraging other women to gain control of their financial lives.

When we first started The Rich Dad Company, Robert, Kim, and I knew that the best way to build the Rich Dad brand would be to focus on Robert as the spokesperson for the brand. He was, still is, and will continue to be the 'celebrity' and best-selling author behind Rich Dad. Kim and I both willingly chose to support him "on the sidelines" in building the company to where it is today. With more than 23 Rich

Dad titles in more than 45 languages, sales of Rich Dad products in 96 countries, and *Rich Dad Poor Dad* on *The New York Times'* bestseller list for over five years, we felt it was time to set new goals for our company and ourselves.

Within the last year Robert said to Kim and me many times, "Thank you both. You have helped me achieve my dreams, now it is your turn. It is time to focus on what each of you is passionate about." 'Rich Woman' is being launched with this book about women and investing and Kim and I plan to expand on these topics with other 'Rich Woman' books. Later this year we will launch 'Rich Family' with a book I am writing.

Kim's passion is encouraging all women to become financially independent. My passion is helping parents educate their children so all children will be able to not only survive, but thrive, in the financial world they will face.

As you read this book, you will most likely recognize yourself in one of the characters Kim introduces. She addresses the many excuses that we women give ourselves and others about WHY we choose not to invest.

"My husband will take care of me."
"I work too hard at my job."
"I want the benefits from a job."
"I don't have the time."
"I don't have the money."
"I am not smart enough."
"My children need me."
"I don't want to be bothered."

Kim addresses each of these excuses and how you can overcome them.

You don't get married expecting to get divorced. Many women end up staying in unhappy and unhealthy relationships because of money.

In a job, the more successful you become, the busier you are, and the less time you have for other endeavors. The more successful you become in investing, the more free time you will enjoy. Your investments will be working hard for you, providing the money you need, instead of you working hard for money.

Within the last few weeks I have lost my father and a dear male friend. Both my mother and my girlfriend now find themselves alone and afraid. They are both very smart and were working women before they were married. Now they must re-train themselves on how to manage their money. This just emphasizes why women need to learn to invest.

Life brings unexpected and unanticipated challenges to all of us. This book will show you how you can depend on yourself through any challenge. Regardless of where you have come from, what your education was, how much money you currently have, or what your excuse may be, this book will show you the kind of courage it takes to change your life.

What better way to learn than through experience? Kim shares the fears she faced as she started investing, how she overcame that fear, and ultimately built her own financial empire that is independent of Rich Dad. You may be a mother recently divorced, or a single woman facing her aging days alone, a recent widow, or a happily married woman worried about having enough money for retirement. You are not alone.

Often it is that first step that is the most difficult. By taking control of your own financial future you will find the self-confidence to help you in all areas of your life. It is through greater self-confidence that you will find the freedom to be, to do, and to have whatever you want.

INTRODUCTION

Why A Book Just For Women?

In the world of investing, the *how* to invest – how to buy a rental property, how to choose a stock, or how to get a good return on your investment – is the same for women as it for men. Whether stocks, bonds, or real estate, investments do not care if it is a man or a woman who is doing the buying, selling, holding, remodeling, or renting.

So why is there a need for a book on investing, just for women?

The answer is because *when it comes to money*, men and women are different – historically, psychologically, mentally, and emotionally.

These differences are at the heart of the reason why so many women today are in the dark when it comes to money and investing. These differences are what separate the sexes and why this book is dedicated to women.

I Hate Being Told What To Do!

The subtitle for this book comes straight from my heart. My husband, Robert, and some friends of ours were having lunch one afternoon, and the subject of this book came up. *Rich Woman* was clearly the title. We hadn't yet decided upon the subtitle. We threw some ideas around the table.

Then Robert turned to me and asked, "Tell me, why are you so driven to be financially independent? This is not something new for you; you've always had this in you. This comes from your core. What is your reason? What is at the heart of this issue for you that you must, come hell or high water, be able to make it on your own? Tell us what drives you."

My girlfriend Suzi was sitting next to me. She and I are extremely like-minded. So much so, that we looked at one another and almost simultaneously declared, "I just hate being told what to do!" The two of us immediately got on our soapboxes about how much we can't stand it and went into example after example of times people told us what to do and how we reacted and why we will never let someone else dictate our lives.

(I know there are a lot of women who understand exactly what I'm talking about. You may even be one of those women.)

We stopped talking. I looked around the table, and everyone was silent, and they were all smiling. "It looks like you have your subtitle," Robert said.

Since I Was Young

This is not a new issue for me. I knew I had a problem following orders even back in kindergarten! No one in my class spent more time out in the hallway than I did. Today it's called a 'time-out.' I didn't want to take a nap; I wanted to play with my friends – out to the hallway. I wanted to finger paint, not listen to a story – out to the hallway. And please don't make me eat that horrible cafeteria food – I know, go stand in the hallway.

The teacher said I was "willful." I just didn't like being told what to do.

I was fired *twice* from my first full-time job out of college – twice from the same job! It wasn't that I was lazy or incompetent, just the opposite. I was so eager to learn. Which is why I was re-hired the second time. But my natural instincts could not be suppressed. I was just a bit too independent, and at age 21, I, of course, knew all the answers. That, coupled with my distaste for taking orders, was not a good recipe for my future success with that company.

This issue was so ingrained in me that when someone would strongly tell me to do something, even though I knew it really would be best for me to do it, I wouldn't do it, just because I didn't want to be told what to do.

Yes, this has caused a few problems in my life… and it has also caused me to be highly independent, especially financially independent.

You may have heard the saying, "He who has the money makes the rules." In my mind the person who has the money can tell others what to do. So I decided early on to be the one making the rules, not being told what to do.

The Stupid Things We Women Do

Robert walked into the house one afternoon to find me yelling at the television, "Wake up! Don't be a fool! Stop acting like a silly little girl! Grow up!"

Robert was laughing at me. "What's going on?"

I said in pure frustration, "It drives me absolutely crazy to see women do such stupid things when it comes to money! This woman is asking a total stranger, some financial planner on TV promoting himself, what to do with a few thousand dollars she has saved up. He's giving her bad advice, and she just says, 'Oh, thank you so much. That's just what I'll do.' How stupid is that? She's a good example of why women are often stereotyped when it comes to money and investing."

"She certainly struck a chord in you," Robert grinned. "Maybe women aren't even aware of what they're doing. Here's your chance to point it out to them."

A List of Silly Things

It definitely did strike a chord in me. Because we women truly do some ridiculously stupid things in our lives – all revolving around money. I think it's time we simply get smarter on the subject.

Am I saying women are stupid? Absolutely not. Nothing could be further from the truth. I am saying that we do some incredibly foolish things. And most of these silly things are directly related to money.

My point is to stress how essential it is to be prepared for whatever might happen. And to encourage you to tell yourself the truth about who or what you are depending upon for your financial future.

Here is a list of a few of the stupid things that many of us women do when it comes to money.

- We marry for money.
- We stay in a bad marriages or relationships because we're afraid we can't make it financially on our own.
- We let a man make all our key financial decisions.
- We accept the myth that men are better with money.
- We accept the myth that men are better at investing.
- We won't challenge a man's financial decisions because we don't want to rock the boat and hurt his ego.
- We take financial advice from supposed "experts" because we don't think we're smart enough.
- We keep quiet to keep the peace.
- We hang on too long because (at least financially) we're "comfortable."
- We're left behind for younger women… because we hung on too long.
- We hope the man will change.
- We settle for "OK" in life when what we really want is "Great."
- A man is lost but won't ask for directions… and we follow him.
- We sell ourselves short.
- We put up with all the inequalities on the job, for a paycheck.
- We feel guilty working extra hours and not being with our kids.
- We get passed over for a promotion we deserve… and stay.
- We accept less pay than our male equivalents and often end up doing their work.
- We miss our kids' soccer games and recitals because we have to work.
- We often look into the future and think, "Someday…"

Most of us have done one or more of these stupid things. The bottom line is that many of us sell our souls in the name of money. The real crime is the toll it takes on our self-esteem, our confidence, and our self-worth.

Yes, this book is about women and investing, but it's actually about much more than that. It's about women taking control of their lives. It's about dignity. It's about self-respect.

A Man, Family, Company, Or Government

The original subtitle of this book was "For Women Who Insist on Being Financially Independent… and not depending upon a man, family, company, or government to take care of them." This truly is the essence of what this book is about. Throughout history women were taught and expected to be financially dependent on someone else for their financial well-being. Today that could be a dangerous position in which to be. Times have definitely changed.

A Man

Historically, it's impossible to talk about men, women, and money without talking about sex. Sex, money, and women are closely interwoven, and often we don't even see the impact one has on the other because we've been raised for generations to accept this as the standard in society.

By the time we are 16, some even younger, we as women, or girls, are aware of the tremendous power we have over men – the power of sex. While most teenage boys are still awkward and goofy, acting like puppies with big feet, we girls begin to notice that boys as well as men begin to look at us differently… they begin to look at us sexually. Often when we are very young, we begin to notice that grown men will smile at us, some will whistle, some will make obvious advances, and others will just stare and drool.

I'm sure we can each recall "that girl" in our class, the one who was more "developed" than the rest of us. In my class it was Melody. At age 14 she knew she was different, that she had an *advantage* over the rest of us girls, and she flaunted her newfound sexuality. When we were in 8th grade, Melody was dating high school juniors and seniors. And in high school she was working the college crowd. She knew how to get all the attention she wanted from men.

Now I realize that Melody is the exception, not the norm. Yet most of us, if we're honest, will admit to knowing exactly how powerful our youthful sexuality could be. A little flirting could go a long way.

It is this sexual need that men have that gives us women such immense power early on, and begins to shape our views about what to do and how to act to get what we want in the world. And the formula works… as long as we are young and sexually attractive. But time marches on, and things change.

A Turning Point

I am 14 years old. I come home from school one day, walk through the front door and hear my mom talking with one of her best friends in the dining room. As I walk toward them Mom sees me out of the corner of her eye and signals me to not approach and let them have their privacy. I walk into the kitchen to get a snack. While pulling the milk carton out of the refrigerator I can't help but overhear their conversation.

It's clear that my mom's friend Gloria was very upset. "I knew we had our problems," she said. "But, because of our kids, I didn't think he'd really leave me."

"What did he say?" Mom asked.

"He said he's been seeing a woman in the city – a much younger woman – for the past year," she said. "According to him, she makes him feel like a hero. Apparently I make him feel like a disappointment."

"Did you know about this affair?" Mom asked.

"To be honest, I suspected something was going on, but I really didn't want to know. I just hoped that it was a fling and that things would eventually return to normal."

"So deep down you knew?" Mom prodded.

"Yes, I guess I did. I just didn't want to admit it to myself," Gloria confessed. "For years our marriage has not been very good. Over the years we had less and less in common. He had his career, and I had the kids. He traveled on business, and I stayed at home."

"So if your marriage wasn't working and you knew he was having an affair, then why did you stay?"

"Because of the kids," Gloria replied quickly.

"The kids?" Mom asked, surprised. "Gloria, your kids are all grown. Your son just graduated college. There's got to be more to it than that."

Gloria hesitated and then quietly said, "I didn't leave because of money. Even though the marriage wasn't good, at least I was taken care of financially. It scared me to think that I'd be out there on my own. I haven't worked for 20 years. I don't know if I can make it on my own. Yes, our marriage has been falling apart for years, but my one saving grace was that at least I was OK financially."

I heard Gloria start to cry. "I just don't know what I'm going to do. It's frightening to face the reality of being 45, on my own, and having to provide for myself. I never dreamed I'd be in this situation."

I put the milk carton back in the refrigerator and went to my room. As I walked up the stairs I heard my mom's friend say, "I just don't know if I can take care of myself financially." Those words really struck a cord in me.

I thought to myself, "Here is this woman in a miserable marriage, and she puts up with it because she is so dependent on her husband to provide for her." At that point I realized that life isn't necessarily the happily-ever-after fairy tale I believed it to be. I remember making a decision that day and saying to myself,

"I will never be dependent on a man, or anyone, for that matter, for my financial life."

And that decision has guided me throughout my life.

It May Be Time To Change The Formula

Please know I am not anti-men. I love men. I just do not want to be financially dependent on them. And so many women are today.

Too often I meet women in their 40s or 50s who are divorced and struggling. The story is pretty much the same: "We were so happy when we were young. Then we grew apart. And he left me for a younger woman. For the first time in my life I am on my own."

I am very fortunate. My mom and dad have been wonderful role models for me in marriage. They have been married for more than 50 years, and I look up to them as examples and teachers of how to have a loving, lasting, and respectful marriage.

Unfortunately many marriages do not pass the test of time. The divorce rate is up; one out of two marriages ends in divorce. I'm not saying plan on a divorce. I am saying be realistic and set yourself up financially to succeed no matter what happens. For Gloria, she had no "plan B." She had one plan – stay married at all costs in exchange for a comfortable material life.

The formula of using our youth and sex appeal to get the attention and influence we desired in order to get what we wanted, worked well for many of us in our 20s and 30s, but it is not the formula to get us what we want in our 40s, 50s, and 60s. It's a waste of time to think men will change. It's time for us women to change. The formula that worked for us when we were young loses its affect as we get older. And for many of us it's time to change our formula. And money plays a key role in the equation. Whereby sex gave us power when we were young, money puts us in control as we get older.

Katherine Hepburn summed it up best. She said:
> *"Women, if you're given a choice between money*
> *and sex appeal, take the money. As you get older,*
> *the money will become your sex appeal."*

The times have changed in more ways than one, and we women need to change with them. That is what this book offers – a roadmap to change. If you are convinced that your best financial strategy is to have a man provide for you until the day you die, then I wish you well. For the rest of us, who are ready to make some changes in our lives, who want more control over our lives and who are ready to take action, I offer an alternative.

A Family

Some of us have the luxury of being able to count on the wealth of our families to carry us through the years. But that certainly is not the majority. Several of my friends, instead of depending on their families to take care of them are now the ones taking care of their families. One girlfriend in Honolulu took her ill mother into her home when her mother couldn't care for herself anymore and became her primary care giver. Not only was the cost of caring for her mother expensive, but she also lost quite a bit of income from her job because of the time she had to take off to be with her mother.

Another friend is paying $8,000 per month for her mother's nursing home expense. She had never planned on being in this situation.

A woman in Scottsdale recently inherited the family home when her mother passed away. Her parents had lived in that home for 30 years. The problem was that the home appreciated so much in value over those 30 years that when the woman inherited the home she also inherited a huge property tax bill. The woman could not afford to pay the taxes due on the house, and, as a result, had to sell the family home is order to pay the taxes, leaving her with next to nothing of her inheritance.

Here is one more scenario that a woman, Susan, shared with me recently that is actually becoming more and more common. Susan's father had amassed substantial holdings in real estate, businesses, and stocks in his lifetime. Susan's mother passed away, and her father remarried. Her father became terminally ill, and while he was in the hospital, close to death, his new wife had his will amended to award all of his holdings to her side of the family. She completely removed Susan and her brother and sister from the will. When Susan's father passed away, Susan got nothing of her wealthy father's estate.

My point in these examples is not to dwell on everything that could go wrong. My point is to stress how essential it is to be prepared for whatever might happen. And to encourage you to tell yourself the truth about who or what you are depending upon for your financial future.

What is occurring within companies and governments will highlight additional reasons why depending upon your family for your financial support may not be your optimum choice.

A Company Or A Government

The October 31, 2005 issue of *TIME Magazine* ran the cover story with the headline – *The Great Retirement Ripoff.* The subtitle states, "Millions of American who think they will retire with benefits are in for a NASTY SURPRISE. How corporations are picking people's pockets – with the help of Congress." The article explains how major U.S. companies have used up or literally stolen the pensions of its workers out from under them. Government legislation allowed companies to simply walk away from the promises they made to their employees to provide monthly retirement payments and healthcare benefits throughout the employees' retirement years.

The article went on to state, "A *TIME* investigation has concluded that long before today's working Americans reach retirement age, policy decision by Congress favoring corporate and special interests over workers will drive millions of older Americans – *a majority of them women* – into poverty, push millions more to the brink and turn retirement years into a time of need for everyone but the affluent."

Here is what grabbed my attention when I read this article. The writer highlighted five case studies of people who had fallen victim to the pension problem. *Every one* of the five cases was a woman. One 69-year-old woman was cut off from her $1,200 monthly pension check, which she was granted as a result of her husband's death while working on the job. Today she collects aluminum cans to generate an extra $60 per month to survive.

Another woman, 60 years old, worked for the Polaroid Corporation for 35 years starting as a file clerk and worked her way into the executive boardroom. She participated in an employee stock-ownership plan (ESOP). She gave up eight percent of her salary to pay for this plan with the expectation that she would have thousands in retirement when she cashed in her shares. The company's shares plummeted in value and because of poor business decisions and intervention by Congress this woman lost between $100,000 and $200,000. On top of that she was expecting tens of thousands of dollars in pension payments and benefits. When all was said and done she received a one-time check of $47.

The five women featured in this article all thought they were set to be financially secure in their retirement years, and now they face poverty. This is outrageous. And there does not appear to be any indication of the pension system being resurrected in the future. It will likely become a thing of the past.

And this is not just happening to women, it is happening to countless husbands and family members as well. This crisis is not gender-specific.

So, again, if you're counting on your husband or family for your financial lifeline take this into account.

The Government – As far as the government is concerned both the Social Security system and the Medicare system are basically bankrupt. I don't know if they will ever be able to turn that problem around. Most surveys indicate that men and women in their 20s and 30s are already aware there may not be Social Security or Medicare available for them when they retire. As with pension plans, the government is unable to honor the promises it has made to those who have contributed to Social Security and Medicare for all their working lives.

It's Your Choice

So a man, family, company, or government may be there for you in the future… I just wouldn't *count* on it. I would not stake my entire financial future on something over which I do not have full control.

It simply comes down to making a decision – do I seek financial independence for myself or financial dependence? It is a conscious choice. If you choose financial *dependence* then know that you are agreeing to allow someone else in your life to be responsible for your financial well-being… and accept the good and the bad consequences that go along with that.

If, on the other hand, your choice is financial *independence* then you are choosing long-term freedom over short-term comfort. You're deciding on the harder road up front – the road from which many women turn away – in order to have the easier, rewarding road in the future.

I am certain that any woman who truly commits to taking control of her own financial life will succeed. Women are doing it every day.

> *This book is about **financial** independence because*
> *I believe the key to freedom for women lies first*
> *in women becoming **financially** free.*

Chapter One

LUNCH WITH THE GIRLS

"I am a woman above everything else."
– Jacqueline Kennedy Onassis

I love New York City. It truly is a one-of-a-kind fabulous city – so much energy, so much activity, never a dull moment. I waved down a cab and the driver pulled over and picked me up at 51st Street near Times Square. The streets were crowded as usual with businesspeople on their way to meetings, street vendors selling watches, purses, and roasted chestnuts, window shoppers eyeing the displays, and hungry men and women on their way to lunch. Which is where I was heading. "Where to?" the driver asked. "The Plaza Hotel," I replied. It was a gorgeous, crisp, cool day – lots of blue sky and a little wind blowing making the air feel just a bit cooler.

The ride to the hotel was shorter than I anticipated. "That'll be $5.70," the driver announced as he pulled up to the main entrance. As I stepped out of the cab I felt a little nervous and excited at the same time. I flew all the way from Phoenix to New York City for one lunch. I had no idea what to expect and, to be honest, I wasn't even sure, just who exactly I was having lunch with. I determined that this lunch could be wonderful or it could be a big mistake. But one thing was sure, it would definitely not be boring.

The e-mail I received two months prior read,

Hi Girls!

OK. We did it! We have the date, time, and place for our girls reunion lunch. We are all meeting on March 22 at 12 o'clock noon at The Plaza Hotel in New York City for lunch! From Honolulu to New York City… yes times have changed. Can't wait to see everyone and hear all of your stories.

With love, Pat

Pat and I were college friends back at The University of Hawaii. We met in a philosophy class and shared an apartment together one year. We hadn't seen each other in about 20 years. Pat decided it was time to reunite our "Hawaii group."

Our Hawaii group was made up of six close girlfriends. We all met during our *memorable*, to say the least, days in Honolulu. We were young, single and living in the Islands. We were having the times of our lives.

We don't know how Pat did it, but she pulled it off. Pat tracked down the five of us (who were now living in different cities throughout the U.S.), organized schedules, chose a location, and set the date for a Hawaii group reunion. We had all pretty much lost touch with one another so this was no small feat. Some of us were married with new last names. All of us had left Honolulu. I know I had moved several times, and I'm sure others had too. But leave it to Pat, Miss Organized, to work her magic and make this event happen.

The last time we were all together was at a lunch in Honolulu 20 years before. We were all starting our careers, and we all had larger-than-life dreams. We all did a lot of growing up together in Honolulu. I was fascinated to see what everyone was up to… and how their lives had unfolded.

I walked up the red-carpeted steps of the hotel entrance. The doorman held the door open for me, and as I walked into the foyer of the hotel it felt as if time had stood still. I immediately recognized Pat and Leslie standing ten feet in front of me. Pat was flawlessly put together, not one hair out of place even as she took off her hat. Her outfit was perfectly matched. Her boots looked brand new, as did her matching gloves. Every detail attended to. She was always like that. She reminded me of the meticulous Felix Unger in the TV show *The Odd Couple*.

Pat always demanded that everything be just so. This is why she arrived almost an hour early that day. She wanted to make sure that everything was exactly as she requested for our reunion. Yes, Pat is the one to call to organize anything. Of course, she'll also drive you crazy at the same time addressing every minute detail.

Leslie stood next to Pat. It was obvious she was still the artist. Dressed in colorful layers – a long loose skirt, bright print shirt, vest, scarf, oversized coat – everything flowing… almost the complete opposite of Pat. Leslie looked like she just flew in with the wind. And I wondered what I'd find in the large overstuffed purse hanging off her shoulder. Being the artist you never knew what to expect of Leslie. She would come across flighty and a bit ditzy, but in actuality she was quite bright. If she was working on a painting of a building built in the 1800s she'd learn the history of the building, of the era, of the artists of that era and their painting styles. She truly loved her art and she embodied it.

We gave each other big hugs and all three of us started yakking immediately. We didn't even notice that we had been ranting on for almost 20 minutes when Janice came flying through the door, direct from the West Coast. Huffing and puffing, completely out of breath, a bit ruffled, she took one look at us and let out a shriek! "It's so great to see you! Can you believe we're all together in New York?" she cried. "It took me forever to get across town! Plus my meeting ran late. Isn't it a beautiful day outside?" Janice blurted out without ever taking a breath. Pat, Leslie,

The last time we were all together was at a lunch in Honolulu 20 years before. We were all starting our careers, and we all had larger-than-life dreams. We all did a lot of growing up together in Honolulu…

and I silently nodded to each other as if to say some things (or people) never change. Janice's entrance was the Janice we all knew and loved. She always had ten things going on at once. She talked fast. She walked fast. She had boundless energy. And she never made a quiet entrance into a room.

We talked for a few more minutes and then the four of us started toward the hostess when Pat's cell phone rang. "That's a shame," we heard Pat say. "It sounds like you'll be working through the night. Thanks so much for making the effort. I'll fill you in on everything. Take care."

"Tracey can't make it. She's on a deadline on a project she's been working on all month. She thought she had it completed, but this morning her boss made a significant change in the project so she can't get away," Pat reported. "I'll tell you, Tracey has put in her time and worked her way up the corporate ladder. Unfortunately, like today, her career often takes precedence over her life. She said she really wanted to be here."

"Where is she living?" Leslie asked.

"Chicago. She works for a large mobile phone company," Pat answered.

The hostess led the way to our table. Pat arranged for a wonderful table in a corner of the room. She even had a small box of chocolate-covered macadamia nuts at each of our settings to commemorate our days in Hawaii. And to our great surprise, at each place she had a framed photo of us all from our last group get-together 20 years ago in Honolulu. We all knew this was going to be an unforgettable lunch.

In gazing at the photo we were each very adamant that we hadn't changed a bit in looks. "And I'm sure our bathing suits would fit us perfectly today as they did then," Janice said sarcastically as we all let out a groan.

"Where is Martha? Is she coming?" I asked as our water glasses were filled. Pat responded, "She was hoping to join us, but she had to cancel at the last minute. Martha said her mother is not well, and she didn't feel comfortable leaving her alone for three days. From what I gathered, her father passed away years ago, so it's just Martha and her mom. She never had brothers or sisters. She said to send her love to everyone."

"Well, four out of six is pretty good," Janice chimed.

Just then our waiter approached with a champagne bucket in one hand and a chilled bottle of champagne in the other. Pat thought of everything. Glasses were put on the table. The champagne was popped and carefully poured into each of our glasses.

"I propose a toast!" Pat announced. "To wonderful friendships that last through the years." We held up our glasses and toasted to one another.

Then we settled back for a long, leisurely lunch.

Chapter Two

THE GIRLS

"Remember, Ginger Rogers did everything Fred Astaire did, but she did it backwards and in high heels."
– Faith Whittlesey

The conversation never let up for a minute. We had one-on-one conversations going then the whole group would join in. We were talking across the table to each other and sideways. We had a lot to catch up on.

Janice, voted the loudest of the group, yelled across to Leslie, "So, Leslie, tell me what you've been doing for the past 20 years." The power of her voice caught everyone's attention, and we all stopped talking and turned to listen to Leslie's answer.

Leslie's Story

Leslie started, "Remember at our last Hawaii lunch I was considering leaving Honolulu in search of more opportunity?" We all nodded. "Well, I moved to New York City about six months later. I figured I might as well go to where the action was; that it would be my best chance at breaking into the commercial art world. I was fortunate to land a job right away with a small graphic design firm. That gave me time to get to know the city and to figure out what I really wanted to do. I was a little shaky at first – moving to New York from Hawaii was a shock. I'd never even been on a subway before. And I learned early on to carry my high-heeled shoes, not walk in them. I had several jobs after that, including working in the art department of Bloomingdales and Macy's.

"In my spare time I always painted. I set up a corner in my tiny apartment as my art studio with my easel and paints. My favorite thing to do was to pack up my supplies and choose a spot in the city, like Central Park or Rockefeller Center, and paint for hours. A few years ago I even had my own showing at a gallery in the city. That was a highlight for me. The show didn't make me a lot of money, but I did sell a few pieces, and it was a thrill just to have my work featured.

"Then I met Peter, the man of my dreams. Peter was a fellow artist. We fell in love, and we married one year later. We have two children together – a boy and a girl. But two artists living together was not an easy match. Definitely not the dream I had envisioned. He had a studio in the city where he would paint, and he did OK for himself selling his paintings and teaching art classes. But I think the problem was that we were too similar. I mean we're artists! We're both spontaneous, not very structured, and neither of us could balance a checkbook. But we could certainly spend money. Our marriage lasted six years. We parted friends.

"Since then I've pretty much been raising our two kids on my own. Peter helps out a little financially, but he doesn't make much money. My daughter is 14, and my son is 12. Today I paint when I can, which actually isn't very often. I work in an art gallery here in the city just down the street. It's been a struggle being a single mom. The cost of living is so expensive in Manhattan, so we moved to New Jersey where we can afford a better lifestyle and the kids have decent schools. So all-in-all it's working out alright, but it's certainly not the life I had planned when I was in my 20s."

"I can't imagine raising two kids by myself," Janice jumped in. "I can barely take care of myself! That's probably why I'm still single. And the cost of living in L.A. can be expensive but not like New York City. I give you a lot of credit, Leslie."

"Thanks," Leslie replied.

"How's life in L.A.?" Pat inquired, looking at Janice. "I've never spent much time in California."

Janice's Story

"I love L.A.," Janice began. "I guess more than that, I really enjoy my business – most of the time. As I said, I never did the marriage thing. I came really close about eight years ago, but just before we were about to mail out the wedding invitations he announces to me he has to 'find himself' and takes off for Europe! He finally writes me about six months later to tell me that he doesn't think he's ready to get married. As if I didn't already figure that out by then! The last I heard he had moved to Bali or Fiji and was living with some 20-year-old. I guess he finally 'found himself.' I haven't been eager to go down that road since. And today, as I get older, dating isn't as easy as it used to be. I see more and more older men with younger women. How do you compete against that?

"So my work is my focus. I continued working with that couple I started with in Honolulu. Remember, they had a tropical gift business? When I began with them they had one shop in Honolulu. They grew their business to three stores in Honolulu, one in Maui, and one on the Big Island. Then their direct mail business to the Mainland exploded. I worked with them for about five years. I had a decent amount of money saved, so I decided to take the plunge and start something on my own. Since I understood the retail business I thought that would be my best bet. I can do this on my own, I thought.

"Well I found out how wrong I could be. My bright idea was to open a small gourmet food store. I only knew of one in Honolulu, and it was doing a great business. I took all the money I had saved plus I got a small business loan, rented a small space just outside Waikiki on a busy street, bought my inventory, and opened my doors. I was sure people would flock through the front door. After sitting in my shop for four days with no customers my first realization hit me – I never told anyone I was there. I just assumed people would show up. Then I learned the difference between selling non-perishable goods and selling food. I also found out the hard way that my rental agreement had a stiff penalty for paying the rent late.

"I came close to quitting several times. Instead I called my former boss and asked for help. At first she laughed. 'Welcome to the world of entrepreneurship!' she said. 'Tell me what's happening.' She became a great mentor to me and helped me turn around my business. I don't think I'd have ever made it had she not given me so much guidance.

"Slowly but surely my business began to pick up. I was so excited when I took out my first 'help wanted' ad. Finally I had enough sales to hire someone to help me. After my first store caught on I opened a second. That store struggled in the beginning as well but eventually both stores grew to have steady sales and decent profits. "

"Then I started to get antsy and I came up with another one of my brilliant ideas – a high-end specialty shop of products for women to pamper themselves with. The store has a soothing environment, and we have a whole range of products from bath oils and candles to services where our salesperson will arrange for dinner to be delivered to a customer's home.

"So I sold my stores in Hawaii and took my concept to California. 'Piece of cake!' I thought." Janice took a deep sigh and paused. "I just about lost everything. Business in L.A. was totally different from business in Honolulu. The rules are different. The products people want are different. The whole attitude is different. It was like starting from scratch. I learned a ton, and to make a long story short, today I have three stores: two in L.A. and one in San Diego. I geared the store to women, but it's becoming really popular with men now. And I'm focusing a lot of my energy on the Internet and having on-line shops as well. What a world that is!"

"It's a lot of work. I have 12 employees in all, and that's a whole other story. I'm constantly back and forth between L.A. and San Diego and then, of course, I'm on the road on buying trips, trade shows, meetings, and conventions to keep improving my business. I'd like to say I'm making a fortune but the truth is so much of what I make goes back into my business," Janice confided. "I love my work, but I do look

We toasted: "To choices! May we all make the most of those that we've made and make good ones for the years to come!"

forward to the day when I can just sit back and watch the money roll in. It is certainly taking a lot longer than I anticipated.

"I look back on how much I've been through in the past 20 years, and it seems like an eternity. Then I remember our carefree days in Honolulu, and that seems like just yesterday. Can we go back there?" Janice said.

We immediately began reminiscing about how we all met, about all the parties on the beaches, the guys, our trips to the outer islands, our first jobs, the guys, the local foods we missed the most, the skimpy bathing suits, the best happy hours… oh, and the guys.

Leslie asked, "Pat, I remember your first job. You were so excited about working for that newspaper. We could never shut you up when you'd start to talk about the stories you were working on. Are you still writing?"

Pat's Story

Pat loved writing. And she loved current affairs. Pat majored in political science and journalism. She knew early on that she wanted to travel the world as a foreign correspondent, writing about global events. After graduating from the university she only sent out two resumes – to the two top newspapers in Honolulu. When she was asked what she would do if she didn't get hired, she replied, "I've prepared for this interview for over four years. If they say no I won't stop until they say yes.

Pat was typically somewhat reserved, unless she was digging deep into a news story. You could find her at her desk surrounded by stacks of books, magazine, and newspapers. She was always searching for facts and was truly a news junkie. She subscribed to five different newspapers and had the news channels on night and day. If you ever wanted to know what was going on in the world, you could ask Pat. She possessed a certainty that we all admired. She knew what she wanted and where she was going.

But sometimes life interferes with our dreams.

"I was doing really well at the newspaper," Pat started. "They were giving me more and better assignments. I was right on track with my plan both professionally and personally. I met my husband, Grant, about three years after I started at the newspaper. We both had big dreams.

"Grant was offered a fantastic opportunity in Dallas with one of the largest banks in the country. He asked me to marry him, and I said yes. I knew I would miss Hawaii and the challenge of my work but this opportunity for him made so much sense for us financially. The next thing I knew we were packed and on our way to Dallas. I had no concerns about getting a job with one of the Dallas papers but then the unexpected happened. I found out I was pregnant. Completely unplanned."

We all joked that we found it hard to believe that anything in Pat's life could ever possibly be "completely unplanned." That was so not Pat.

"Maybe so," she continued, "but just try finding a job when you're pregnant! I guess I was kidding myself to think it wouldn't be hard. But it definitely was. I know one interviewer was thinking when I told him I was pregnant, 'Why are we even wasting our time? I'll train you and then you'll leave here in six or seven months.' It seemed no one was too anxious to hire a pregnant woman back then, much less a mother with a newborn. So that threw me for a loop. I did some writing on the side, but we pretty much depended on Grant's income. It was frustrating and discouraging. It really set me back.

"We figured since we wanted two or three children that we might as well have them now and then once they were a little older I would resume my journalism career. Well, a few years grew into several. I became a stay-at-home mom with three wonderful children. Grant was promoted several times and today is a top executive making really good money, so I can't complain. We never really needed the money from a second job, so I never did make my way back to the news desk. Now that two of our three kids will soon be entering college I feel like I finally have the time to devote to my writing, but so much has changed in the news world and I've lost so much time and momentum over the years, I'm not sure I have the energy to do what it takes to get back in the game."

What was the noisiest table in the restaurant was now quiet. We could pick up the sound of regret in Pat's voice. We were awkward and silent. None of us knew what to say next. Then Pat looked up from her glass and said, as if to read our minds, "Look, we all have choices, and I made mine. Are there some things I would have done differently? Sure. But all in all I chose motherhood over my career, and I do not regret that," she ended firmly.

Pat was crystal clear, and her comment relieved the tension at our table, which prompted Janice to raise her glass. She affirmed, "To choices! May we all make the most of those that we've made and make good ones for the years to come!" We all toasted.

Leslie looking at her empty glass said, "I think we're ready for a little more champagne. And then I want to hear from Kim."

Chapter Three

MY STORY

"If you obey all the rules, you miss all the fun."
– Katharine Hepburn

The waiter overheard Leslie's comment and was immediately at our table refilling our glasses. As soon as he walked away, Leslie asked, "So what's been happening the past 20 years in your life, Kim?"

"It's been quite a ride," I began. "I remember reading a book when I was 13 years old about four men and women, in their late teens, early 20s, who traveled throughout Europe. The story vividly described the adventures they encountered along the way – the good and the bad. Living in New Jersey at the time, where I was born and raised, that book really opened my eyes to the fact that there was a world out there beyond New Jersey, New York, and Pennsylvania. Which is one of the reasons I moved to Hawaii."

"I remember your family living in Oregon," Pat said.

"When I was 14 we moved from New Jersey to Oregon," I replied. "That was my first glimpse that another world existed outside the life I knew growing up. I got a small taste of how much more there is to see in this world, and I decided I wanted to see it."

"So when my parents asked me where I wanted to go to college, I said, 'Hawaii.' I thought that would be a fascinating place to live and explore. Not surprisingly, they questioned how much time I'd spend in the classroom and how much time I'd spend at the beach. Valid point. But knowing that I was not the model student and probably would not thrive in a traditional university, they agreed to the first year… thinking that after one year I'd get "this Hawaii thing" out of my system and then get serious about my education."

"You did leave Hawaii," Pat said. "But you came back."

"Yes, I did," I acknowledged. "Since I wanted to travel, I actually transferred universities five times in four years. I ended up graduating from the University of Hawaii with a degree in marketing. I'm the youngest of three girls in my family, and being that my parents put all of us through college, when I received my diploma I wrapped it up and mailed it to my parents with a note that read, 'Congratulations! You deserve this more than I do.'"

"I remember meeting your parents on a trip they made to Honolulu," Pat said. "They were so fun!"

"I'm very fortunate," I said. "My parents have always been wonderful role models for me. Since I can remember they told me I could accomplish anything I wanted. They encouraged me to think for myself and told me over and over again, 'The most important thing of all is that you are happy.' And they lived what they taught me. My mom, a schoolteacher who taught in the traditional school system as well as teaching special needs children, has always been the great optimist. Through her I learned the meaning of kindness, of caring and of not getting worked up over the small annoyances that come along. 'Is it really worth getting so upset over?' she would ask. "My dad, a businessman and sales pro, was my example of honesty and integrity. He taught me that if I make an agreement with someone, then I should honor that agreement at all costs. Today my parents are both the most supportive and proud of all that Robert and I do."

"And like all of us you loved the islands and stayed," Janice said.

"Let's face it," I said. "We were all young, single, living in Honolulu, with little responsibilities. What's not to love?"

"So true," Janice said. "Those were some very fun times."

My First Job

I continued with my story. "My first full-time job was in the media department of one of the largest advertising agencies in Honolulu. It was a great first job. Because Honolulu is such a small place I got to know the advertising community very quickly. And it was a fun group of people.

One of the first lessons from Rich Dad that Robert shared with me was this: The key to the 'I' or investor quadrant is to have your money working hard for you so that you don't have to work hard for money.

"From the ad agency I went to the other side of the advertising arena and landed a position in advertising sales. This is where I was working when we were last together. As you may or may not remember, sales did not come naturally to me, and I had no training program built into my job. It was strictly on-the-job learning. I was 25 and running a magazine that served the business community of Honolulu. My primary focus was selling ads for the publication. I had two other sales reps working for me. If there were no sales then there was no magazine. With every issue there was pressure to increase the ad sales from the previous issue. We scrambled every month. And every month we pulled it off."

"That's where you were when we had our final Honolulu lunch together. Where did you go from there?" Leslie asked.

"I was with the magazine for about two years, and I decided it was time for a big change. Here was my plan: Step 1: Move to New York City, the advertising Mecca of the world. Step 2: Work my way up the advertising corporate ladder. Step 3: Be rewarded with the corner office on Madison Avenue! That was my plan, and I was sticking to it… or so I thought.

"I quickly realized there was one problem with my plan. I worked out that in order to work my way up the corporate ladder I would have to excel at carrying out orders. I would need to be exemplary at following instructions. And as you all know, I really do not like being told what to do. History has clearly shown that following directions is not my forte. I did mention that I was fired twice from my first job, didn't I?

"So I determined it was time to move to Plan B. I admitted to my character flaw: I'm hopeless at working for someone else. I thought to myself, 'I know what I'll do. I'll be my own boss!'

"This immediately brought me to my next dilemma, which was I knew nothing about starting a business. I hadn't grown up around business owners. I had no idea how to begin? What kind of business did I want? I overwhelmed myself just thinking about it. But at least I knew one thing: I wanted my own business. How to get there was another story. Being a bold 20-something I decided to still move to New York City and figure it out from there."

My First Date With Robert

"I invited my girlfriend Karen to join me at TGI Fridays in Honolulu to talk about my plans to move to the Big Apple," I explained. "We met after our gym workout, and as we were sitting at the bar she spotted her friend Robert who was there with his buddies. We said hello, and that was it… or so I thought.

"To make a long story short, Robert asked me out for almost six months. I kept saying no. I explained that I was moving to New York City, and I couldn't think of the possibility of a new relationship. To thicken the plot it turns out that Karen was an old girlfriend of Robert's from about eight years earlier. So Robert phones my friend Karen and says, 'Karen, I know that you and Kim are best friends. Would you do me a big favor?' Karen said, 'I know you're up to something. What do you want?' Robert, being the salesman that he is, says, 'I want a referral!' 'I knew this wasn't a social call,' Karen laughed.

"Sure enough Karen begins to tell me what a wonderful guy Robert is. The problem is she does such a great job of selling that I'm now convinced that Karen still likes Robert. And being very loyal to my girlfriends, I wasn't about to go out with someone she had strong feelings for. So another two months passed. And I'm still working my plan to move to New York. By this time Karen had convinced me that she was not interested in Robert romantically. Over the months that Robert was in hot pursuit he sent me flowers, postcards from his travels, cards with personal notes, and more flowers. So one afternoon

Robert calls me at work and asks me out again. I am now intrigued and loving the attention, so I say, 'How about tonight?'

"Back to Robert's salesmanship skills. From the many fact-finding calls Robert had with Karen, he discovered my two favorite things – good champagne and walks on the beach. That was all he needed to put his plan in place for our first evening together. As I pull up to the very posh beachfront hotel on the beach of Diamond Head, where Robert lives, the valet opens the door to my little orange Toyota Celica and says, 'You must be Kim; Robert is waiting for you. Let me show you to his apartment.' We walk into the lobby, and I take the elevator to Robert's apartment. He opens the door. I go inside and we talk for a short while. We then go downstairs to Michel's, one of the finest restaurants in all of Honolulu, right on the beach. The maitre d' approaches. 'Mr. Kiyosaki, I have your table ready looking out on the beach, and your champagne is chilling.' OK… I'm impressed. As the champagne is being poured the maitre d' reappears and suggests, 'If you'd like, why don't you take your champagne with you and go for a walk along the water.' OK, enough already. I'm sold. And we've been together ever since."

Business Partners… At First Sight

"We stayed up until 3:00AM talking on that first date. I still remember the key question Robert asked me that night. He asked, 'What do you want to do with your life?' Immediately out of my mouth came the words, 'I want my own business. I'm not very good at taking orders, and I love business, so it seems the solution for me is to have my own business.' His answer was, 'I can help you with that.' Within one month we began our first business venture together. Along with being life partners since that first date, we've also been business partners ever since.

"That night Robert also explained the business model his Rich Dad had taught him. He drew this diagram…"

I took a notecard from my purse and drew the quadrant diagram.

"'I call this the CASHFLOW Quadrant,' Robert said. 'It represents the four types of people found in the world of business. 'E' stands for employee.' S' stands for self-employed. 'B' stands for business owner, and 'I' stands for investor.'

"'Right now I'm an 'E,'" I said. "And when I first saw this quadrant I asked Robert, 'What's the difference between a self-employed person and a business owner?'

"He explained that a self-employed person might be a doctor, accountant, mechanic, or beautician. She owns the business, and she works in the business. 'S's are often the sole income producers in their businesses. A business owner depends on other people working in the business and operates the business with very good systems. Microsoft, Harley Davidson, and Starbucks are examples of 'B's. Here is the difference between the two: If an 'S takes a one-month vacation, then her income stops for one month. When she takes a break, her income takes a break. If a 'B' takes a one-month or a one-year vacation, when she returns her business will be running as well if not better without her. Robert said, 'The key to the I or investor quadrant is to have your money working hard for you so that you don't have to work hard for money.'

"'So ideally I want to move to the 'B' and 'I' side of the quadrant where my business is making me money whether I'm there or not and my investments are doing the same,' I concluded.

"'That's the plan,' Robert said.

"Two months later we started our first business together. We designed a logo with the words "Win/Win" and embroidered it on shirts and jackets and marketed them at various conferences, seminars, and conventions throughout the U.S. The purpose of this first business was to create the income to fund our travel and tuition to these educational programs for one year as we prepared to build our next business."

> *Note: As I talk with women about business and investing, I am encouraging them to move from the 'E' and 'S' side of the CASHFLOW Quadrant to the 'B' and 'I' side. This is where your efforts are most greatly rewarded. (Please read* Rich Dad's CASHFLOW Quadrant *to learn more.)*

1985 – Our Year From Hell

"In December 1984 we sold all we had, which wasn't much, and left Honolulu to begin building our business in Southern California. It didn't take long, about two months to be exact, before we had gone through the money we had. We were broke and without jobs or work. We had a long ways to go before we were ready to launch our business. At times we were even homeless, sleeping in a beat-up Toyota Celica. I can honestly say 1985 was the worst year of our lives."

"What was it like?" Pat asked.

"Have you ever heard someone say, 'Money can't make you happy'? I asked.

"Of course," Leslie said.

"Well I can tell you first-hand that no money can make you miserable. I used to think that rich people were greedy, heartless and mean. But then I found out first-hand that those qualities are by no means reserved for the wealthy. When Robert and I had nothing we argued with each other, blamed one another. Resentment built – we were definitely not at our best. We were stressed beyond belief. The worst part of it all for me was that my self-esteem hit rock bottom. I was always a very optimistic, happy, decisive, confident woman. But when we went through this taxing period I began to question and doubt everything I knew and believed in, including my ability to accomplish anything. I'd ask myself, 'Do I know anything at all?' What started as a few self-doubts quickly spiraled into what seemed like at the time a huge dark hole impossible to climb out of."

"How in the world did you get yourself out of that mess?" Pat asked.

One Night Of Refuge

"Robert and I would actually knock on doors of people we 'sort of' knew and ask if we could stay at their house for the night. There was one night during this horrific period of time the two of us will never forget. Our credit cards were completely maxed out. In those days not everyone had the automatic credit card machines to check on the status of the credit card being used. So one afternoon our friend drove us to the 6-Pence Motel. It was a cheap motel just off the freeway in San Diego. I walked into the lobby and put my credit card down on the counter, keeping my fingers crossed that the man behind the desk wouldn't check my card. He manually took an imprint of my card and handed me a room key. I stopped myself from jumping up and down right there in the lobby. I was almost running as I went out the door toward the car. 'We got a room! We got a room!' I said as loud as I could without being overheard by the hotel clerk.

"To many this was just a cheap motel. To us, that night, it was heaven. We walked across the street to Kentucky Fried Chicken and bought a bucket of chicken and then headed next door to the grocery store and got a six-pack of beer. We went back to our room, finally, just the two of us. For that moment everything was all right. We had some shelter from the storm. That night we just held each other, not knowing what tomorrow would bring, but at least for that one night we were OK."

"I'm certain neither Robert nor I would have come through that year as we did, had we not had each other. All along we both had friends and family saying to us, 'Why don't you get a job?' 'Take the paycheck for a while until your business is up and running.' We knew that getting jobs would be a step backward. We had come this far, let's not quit now. We also knew that if we went for the comfort of the 'paycheck' then we might never build our business. Looking back it was actually being in this horrible situation that was our driving force. It drove us to find a way out of the mess we were in. And the way out wasn't easy, and it wasn't through getting a job. We were determined to build our business."

It's Time We Take Control

I went on. "We finally came to the point where we simply had had enough of this chaos that we created. Robert came to the conclusion that no one was going to make his life better except him and that it was time for bold measures. I decided to stop feeling sorry for myself. I stopped blaming everyone else for my circumstances. And the two of us simply made the decision to take control of our future and to get to work. So we did."

"What was your business?" Janice asked.

"We built an education company focused on entrepreneurship," I replied. "While Robert built several businesses in Honolulu before our move to California, he was studying for years how people learn, and new and innovative methods for teaching. Our business grew to eleven offices in seven countries throughout the world. We were constantly on the road, mostly overseas."

Leslie asked, "When did you two get married?"

"We were married in November 1986 in La Jolla, California," I said. "The business wasn't thriving by any means at that point but we could see a brighter future ahead."

"What happened to that business?" Pat asked. "Do you still have it?"

I explained: "In 1994, after ten years of running the company, we sold it and retired. I was 37 years old. Robert was 47. The best part about it was that we were free."

"Free financially?" Pat asked.

"Yes. We no longer had to work for money." I replied. "It was a great feeling."

Leslie asked: "So you must have sold your company for a lot of money to never have to work again – especially if you were only 37. That means you would have enough money to last for at least 50 or 60 years, or more."

I laughed. "That's what most people think. It wasn't the sale of our company that allowed us to retire. If we had to depend upon that money to live on then we would have probably burned through the money from the sale in about two years."

"I don't understand," Leslie said, confused.

"We were able to retire in 1994 because of our *investments*. Every month we had money coming in from our investments, primarily in real estate, that more than covered our living expenses. That's what I mean when I say we were financially free."

My Very First Investment

"I know nothing about investing," Pat admitted. "That's all foreign to me."

"I didn't either," I said. "When I started down the investor path I honestly did not even know what the word *investing* meant. I had a very steep learning curve ahead of me."

"What did you invest in?" Janice asked.

"I started with real estate. That made the most sense to me. I bought my first rental property in 1989. It was a small, cute two-bedroom, one-bath rental house in Portland, Oregon. It was only two blocks away from where we lived. I have to tell you it was the most frightening thing I had ever faced. I was scared to death. I was worried. I was afraid of making mistakes that would cost us money. I really didn't know what to expect.

"I won't go into all the details now," I said. "But I was ecstatic when after my first month of ownership I received a whopping $50.00 profit, or cash flow, from that property. I was hooked at that moment. Today I control many millions of dollars worth of real estate as well as other investments. And it's through my investments, which throw off ample amounts of cash flow every month, that I am completely financially free and independent today."

Janice said, "When I think of the word 'investing,' I think of mutual funds, or stocks and bonds. I don't typically think of real estate. Do you make your money buying and selling houses?"

"No it's not through buying and selling. It's through buying and holding. But that's a big subject. We can talk about that later if we want."

The Rich Dad Company

"What did you and Robert do after you retired?" Leslie prodded. "I can't imagine you hanging out by the pool every day."

"That definitely wasn't the case," I grinned. "That year we bought an 85-acre ranch in a small town called Bisbee. Bisbee is an artsy community up in the mountains of Southern Arizona. There was a broken down shack on the property that was actually an old stagecoach depot in the days of the wild west. We rebuilt it into a wonderful one-bedroom house with a separate artist's studio on the stream. There was no TV, no radio… only peace and quiet.

"It was in the quiet of Bisbee that Robert wrote the book *Rich Dad Poor Dad*, with the subtitle *What the Rich Teach Their Kids About Money That The Poor and Middle Class Do Not!* While Robert was writing in Bisbee, I was in Phoenix converting a small hotel into an apartment building. This was a first for me, and I'm happy to say it turned out to be a nice success.

"And speaking of success, *Rich Dad Poor Dad* is now one of the top four longest running New York Times bestsellers in history. Before the launch of *Rich Dad Poor Dad* we created a board game called CASHFLOW 101. We designed the board game to teach people specifically what we did to become financially free. By playing the game people get a hands-on experience of both investing, and accounting for, their money. In the game the purpose is to get out of the Rat Race, where most people live every day, and onto the Fast

Track where the bigger investments lie. And the key to getting from one to the other is a thing called cash flow. When your cash flow from your investments is greater than your monthly living expenses then you are out of the Rat Race!

"Robert and I and our business partner, Sharon Lechter, self-published *Rich Dad Poor Dad*. We printed 1000 copies of the book in April 1997. To be honest, we thought we'd have Christmas presents to last us the next ten years. No bookstore wanted the book. No distributor would touch it. No wholesaler would even return our calls. So we began marketing it ourselves. The first place we had the book for sale was in our friend's car wash. We put it wherever we could. The book slowly started to sell. Word of mouth spread and within two years *Rich Dad Poor Dad* was on *The Wall Street Journal's* bestseller list. We were high as kites!

"Frankly we did not set out to build another company, but The Rich Dad Company has now grown beyond our wildest expectations. Today the book is in over 46 languages and in over 97 countries. CASHFLOW 101 is in 16 languages, and counting. There is a complete series of Rich Dad books as well as a series of Rich Dad's Advisors books, written by people who advise us on investing and business. The business has grown and continues to grow into a worldwide brand representing financial freedom and independence. *No one is more overjoyed and grateful than Robert and I.*"

"What a life!" Leslie exclaimed. "You've been through your fill in the past 20 years – from homeless to retired to a highly successful international company. You are so fortunate. I'd love to be in your position today."

"I am definitely fortunate," I acknowledged. "But I don't know if most people would be willing to go through what Robert and I endured to get where we are today. We took the hard road – the road most people avoid – in exchange for what we anticipated would become the easier road in the future. Fortunately that course of action paid off for us.

"So that's my story. One thing is certain, it has not been boring."

A Special Note To Women:

In talking with so many women I've met because of The Rich Dad Company, I'm repeatedly asked, "Will you please talk to women about investing?" That was the impetus for this book. The main purpose of this book is to very simply inspire women to take action and to understand that becoming financially independent is not rocket science. Any one of us can do it. It just takes some time and education.

One point that I trust will be crystal clear throughout this book is this: Today, more than ever, we, as women, can no longer depend on someone else, be it our husband or partner, our parents, our boss, or our government, to take care of us financially. What was true for our mothers and grandmothers is not applicable to us today. In my opinion women must learn to invest to ensure a secure life for themselves and their children. It is no longer just an option. The rules have changed and it's time we take control of our financial futures.

Chapter Four

Twenty Years Ago...
In the Islands

"Women want men, careers, money, children, friends, luxury, comfort, independence, freedom, respect, love, and three dollar pantyhose that won't run."
— *Phyllis Diller*

After hearing what we've each been up to for the past 20 years, we returned to our days together in Hawaii. The "do you remembers?" began to flow.

Pat raised her hand, "Who remembers our last lunch together?"

The table fell silent for about 30 seconds as we instantly transported ourselves back to the islands. None of us grew up in Hawaii. We were all drawn there for the obvious reasons: sandy beaches, great lifestyle, warm ocean waters, the tropical, balmy weather, and fun! fun! fun! My first trip to Hawaii was with my family when I was in high school. I decided on that one-week vacation that the luckiest people in the world lived in Hawaii and that's where I would live.

We all drifted off to our carefree, single days in paradise. Finally Janice broke the silence, "Twenty years ago at the Tahitian Lanai."

Leslie laughed. "It was in January. A gorgeous sunny day. I still remember Janice in her big floppy hat and Martha in her pink polka dot super-skimpy top. The men were tripping over themselves."

"I remember all of us sitting outside, right along the beach. You could smell the suntan lotion, " Pat added. "And it was strictly house wine in those days, not expensive champagne. Those were such great times. No responsibilities, no worries, we were all barely making any money, but we sure lived well."

"And we were all in great shape since we lived in our bathing suits," Janice said.

"We all did a lot of growing up together," I said. "It's too bad that Martha and Tracey couldn't be here today. It would have been so good to have us all together. But, Pat, you did a great job tracking us all down. We owe you one."

Martha's Story

Leslie reminisced, "I remember Martha was *always* in a bathing suit. She always had her surfboard with her at the beach. Yes, she was the ultimate 'surfer girl.' She grew up on the beaches of Southern California. It was no surprise with her love of the ocean and everything connected to it that she went into oceanography."

Janice said, "I remember when we were last together Martha had just started working at the Marine Life Institute. She was in seventh heaven. Her passion had always been to preserve the oceans and the marine life. She was on a mission to save the world! Her dream was to work with Jacques Cousteau on his famous boat, Calypso. Do you know if she ever came close? You spoke with her, Pat."

"I only spoke with her briefly," Pat said. "I asked her why she moved back to California. She said she originally went back to help out in her father's business for a couple months when his top employee suddenly left. But then she said she just stayed. She told me it was easier. And she could surf whenever she wanted. I remember her saying that her life then was 'very comfortable.' But she sounded frazzled when we talked. Apparently her father passed away, and now she and her mother live together. As I mentioned she couldn't join us because her mother was not well, and Martha is the only one to care

"Twenty years have gone by," Pat sighed. *"And my life is almost 180 degrees different than I ever envisioned. What happened?"*

"I think it's called 'life,'" Leslie said. *"Life happened."*

for her. That has to be difficult."

"So she never went back to her oceanography?" I asked.

"Apparently not. She seemed to avoid that subject when I asked her about it," Pat answered.

"That surprises me," I said.

"Did she say if she was married, or if she had kids?" Janice asked.

"She didn't say," Pat responded.

Tracey's Story

"How is Tracey? What's she up to?" I asked.

"She sounded really frustrated when I talked with her earlier today," Pat began. "She was 'bummed' she couldn't be here and, as she put it, 'So sick and tired of the corporate world.' I'm not sure if it was just the moment, the struggles with her current project, or if there was more to it than that. Although even when I spoke with her on a few other occasions she didn't sound all that happy. There was just no lift in her voice. She sounded tired. I know she is married and has two kids. Being an executive in her company plus raising two kids – and a husband – is not an easy road. She's pretty amazing."

"Well it seems like Tracey pursued her ambition," I replied. "She and I met through work... well sort of. Do you remember every Friday night in Honolulu, after work, the city would close off the main streets in downtown? The restaurants all stayed opened late. There were bands playing. The streets were filled with people, mostly those who worked in or around the downtown area. You could wander in and out of one restaurant or bar after another. It was a great place to meet people, definitely one of the benefits of working downtown. That's where I met Tracey. We immediately hit it off. It turned out we both attended the business school at the University."

I went on, "Tracey was really taken with the corporate world. Her plan was to work her way up the corporate ladder, and it sounds like that's exactly what she did. I remember that she got a job straight out of college in an entry level position working for one of the large local food companies and that she was quickly promoted several times to a pretty impressive position. She would tell me about her business trips to the outer islands and how much she loved interacting with clients. She was definitely in her element back then. I trust she still is."

"It's amazing how much has happened in the past 20 years," Pat sighed. "My life is almost 180 degrees different than I ever envisioned when I was first starting out on my own. So many turns I never expected."

"I think it's called 'life,'" Leslie countered. "Life happened." She paused and said, "I don't know if you all remember the conversation we had toward the end of our last lunch together and what led to us being here today." We all admitted we didn't know exactly which conversation Leslie was referring to.

"It went something like this," Leslie recalled. "Janice joined us about a half an hour late, huffing and puffing. Talking a mile a minute about all the things that came up to make her late."

"Some things never change," Pat interrupted.

"Hey! No fair!" Janice laughed.

Our 20-Year Pact

Leslie proceeded to give a vivid account of our long-ago conversation:

"'So what have you all been talking about?' Janice asked as her purse was falling off her shoulder and her big floppy hat was about to blow off her head. 'What have I missed? Fill me in. Fill me in.'

"We all gave her shortened versions of where we were in our conversations. And then Pat said, 'I wonder what we'll all be doing 20 years from now.'

"'Twenty years from now!' Martha cried. 'We can barely think past this lunch, much less 20 years into the future.'

"'In 20 years we'll be old!' Tracey blared. 'Who wants to think about that!?' We all laughed. We didn't want to think, period. We just wanted to enjoy our leisurely lunch with the girls.

"But Pat persisted, 'C'mon, you guys, where do you see yourselves, what do you want to be doing?'

"Janice jumped in, 'I want to be independently wealthy, madly in love, and traveling the world.'

"'I'll take that!'

"'Me too!'

"'Ditto!'

"'Count me in!'

"We were all thinking, 'Whew! That got us out of a lengthy, serious, introspective, deep discussion about our futures. It is too nice a day to think about our futures. It seems like we've been asked that same question ever since we were in grade school – What do you want to be when you grow up? Let's just enjoy today.'

"Still Pat took one last shot at it. 'I'm sure we'll be seeing each other throughout the years, but eventually we'll probably go off in different directions. How about we all agree to get back together in twenty years? Wouldn't it be fun to see what we're all doing then?'

"To get Pat off the subject once and for all we agreed that 20 years from that day we would all come together for a 'girls lunch' and share our lives with one another. Of course there was no discussion of who would organize this and how we would keep in touch up until then. But we'd made the decision, and we could just enjoy lunch."

We all laughed and applauded Leslie's recollection of our beachside conversation. She was right on.

"I remember getting everyone to agree to get back together but I forgot the rest," Pat admitted.

"Just promise me you're not going to get us into deep and heavy thought at this lunch too," Janice insisted laughingly.

"I'll leave that up to one of you this time," Pat said.

"Would anyone care for dessert?" our waiter asked.

It's About More Than the Money

"You can have it all. You just can't have it all at one time."
– Oprah Winfrey

We couldn't resist ordering a couple of desserts to share between the four of us. Once the waiter left with our order, Leslie asked, "Kim, you said you retired several years ago, correct?"

"Yes, in 1994," I responded.

"It sure doesn't sound like you're leading a leisurely, laid-back life today. My picture of retirement is spending time on the golf course at the country club or lounging on the decks of cruise ships. You seem to be working more than ever."

I laughed. "I definitely would not say I have a relaxing life. You bring up a good point though. I think in most people's minds the word 'retire' conjures up those idyllic pictures – a couple lying on a white sand beach, playing 18 holes with golfing pals, or traveling to those faraway places you always dreamed of."

"I like the faraway places and white sand beaches," Janice interjected.

"I do too," I agreed. "I also enjoy a round of golf. And, more importantly to me, I love new challenges, and I love to learn. And my work is such a huge part of my life. My point is that it wasn't so much that I was *retired* or that I stopped working, it was that I was in a financial position in which I no longer *had* to work if I chose not to. I no longer needed the money from my work or business to live on. I

could *choose* to do whatever I wanted. I was literally financially free –
free to do what I wanted."

Leslie kept at it, "So, if you don't mind my asking, how did you get
to that position? I know you said you had money coming in from your
investments, but I don't understand how that alone could be enough to
retire on. I mean, to not have to work you must have made a fortune.
How did you manage that?"

"First of all, I did not make a fortune," I began. "It was a process
that started for us years earlier. Robert's Rich Dad always said to him,
'You have to learn how to have your money work hard for you, so you
don't have to work hard for money.' He said that as long as you were
the one working for the money then you would never be free because
you'd always have to be working to keep the money coming in."

"What do you mean, 'Robert's Rich Dad'?" Janice asked.

"His Rich Dad was his best friend's father, who dropped out of
school at the age of 13 to help provide for his family. He went on to
become one of the wealthiest men in the state of Hawaii. Robert
credits much of what he's learned about money and investing to his
Rich Dad.

"When he was just 9 years old his Rich Dad began teaching him
how to have his money work for him. And that's what I began learning
in 1989. In that year I started to learn how to put my money to work
for me. That's when I was introduced to the world of *investing.*"

"OK, you've mentioned investing several times," Leslie said
impatiently. "I have some real concerns when it comes to investing.
People lose money investing! I think investing is way too risky. And
too confusing! You need the mind of a financial wizard to understand
investing! I'm an artist; I can barely balance a checkbook. I don't think
I could ever get my arms around investing!"

"I've always left the investing up to my husband," Pat said. "I just
don't seem to have a knack for it. It's so complicated. And I can never
understand what the stock brokers are talking about." Then she asked,
"Do you play the stock market? Do you make a lot of money buying

and selling stocks? My husband seems to just break even when he invests."

Janice added, "I own some stocks and mutual funds but I don't pay much attention to them. I bought them years ago. I do the buy-and-hold thing, but it's really like buy-and-hope-they-go-up-in-value. Besides, I'm too busy with my business to bother."

I sat there quietly after they finished their comments. They were all looking to me to respond. I chose my words carefully. "All I said was the word 'investing' and all three of you had automatic reactions. Leslie says it's too risky. Pat says it's too complicated. And Janice doesn't have the time. You're all telling me why investing is not for you."

I went on, "Let's back up a minute. Leslie asked me how I retired. I said through investing. But let me be really clear, my goal was not to invest. My goal was not even to become rich. My goal was to be *financially independent.* I knew early on in my life that I did not want to be dependent on anyone – a husband, a boss, my parents, anyone – for my financial well-being. To me, *financial independence equals freedom.* As long as I was dependent on someone else for my survival I wasn't free. That was very simply it. The way financial independence was defined to me was like this: financial independence came the moment I had more money flowing in every month, without me working for it, than was going out for my monthly living expenses.

"There are many ways to accomplish this," I explained. "Of course there's the lottery but I knew my chances of winning the jackpot were slim to none. I didn't plan on inheriting the money. And I wasn't going to marry for money."

Janice interrupted, "Remember Erica who worked at the health club? She married for money. Married some guy 30 years older than her. Boy does she have some stories to tell. I don't know who's had more affairs, her or him."

We all looked at Janice with blank stares on our faces.

"Sorry, just thought I'd throw that in," she said.

"Like I said, I wasn't going to marry for money," I resumed. "Some people make their fortunes in business. And even as Robert and I built our businesses, there was certainly no guarantee of success. And if our businesses were successful, how long would we want to run them? So when I was introduced to the world of investing I got interested."

Leslie looked confused. "You know, I did react. And as I sit here I now realize that I really don't know what the word investing means."

I smiled. "Like I said, I didn't either. And to be honest it wasn't so much the idea of *investing* that caught my interest, it was this concept of having money coming in every month from my investments that I didn't have to literally show up at work for. As you said earlier, Leslie, any one of us would need a fortune in order to not have to work. And if I was planning on living off of my savings, then I *would* need a fortune in savings. But if instead you have money coming in each month from *investments* you have purchased, then you don't need to acquire a huge lump sum of cash to live off of. Is this making sense?"

All three hesitantly nodded their heads.

"So it's more important to you to have money steadily coming in on a monthly basis rather than to have amassed large amounts in savings?" Pat asked.

"Yes" I replied. "It's called cash flow. Every month the cash flows in."

"How much cash flowing in do you need every month?" Pat asked.

"Great question. Whether or not I work, I want money coming in each month that will pay for all of my living expenses… and then some. That is very simply it. That was the goal from the start. To acquire investments that threw off enough cash flow each month to pay for my lifestyle. And what's so important about that? Because at that point, at age 37, I was free. At that point I no longer *had* to show up at an office, miss out on things I wanted to do, or be told what to do by my boss. At that point I no longer needed to rely on anyone for money. I was free to do what I wanted, when I wanted. I think for me it was the point when I really began to ask myself, 'what do I want to do with my life?' It was somewhat like being back in Honolulu 20 years ago, just starting out and having all these options available to me, only better because I wasn't worried about money. It was now a matter of choosing what I wanted to do because I wanted to do it, not because I *needed* to do it. Financial independence is about having more choices.

"Let me add one more thing. I see so many women who are trapped in miserable marriages because they are financially needy or dependent on their husbands or women who are in jobs they hate because they need that steady paycheck. In my opinion they stay because they've chosen 'security' over 'self-esteem.' That to me is the biggest crime of all. Many women choose an unhappy situation or environment for financial reasons, and then they say, 'Money's not that important.' Money plays a bigger role in women's lives than most of us will admit. Just ask yourself, if you had all the money in the world are there just maybe a few things you'd be doing differently in your life? Money has the power to keep a woman trapped or to set her free. It's up to her."

The three women around the table were silent. I think I got their attention.

> *I got to the point where I asked myself, 'What do you want to do with your life?' Because now I had choices. I could what I wanted to do simply because I wanted to do it, not because I needed to do it.*
>
> *Financial independence is about having more choices.*

Why Women Must Become Investors

A young journalist approached me recently and said quite passionately, "We have to make women aware that they have to take charge of their money. They cannot depend on someone else to do that for them!" After talking with her more I discovered where her passion was coming from. It turns out her 54-year-old mother recently divorced. She was left with basically nothing and had now moved in with her daughter. Her daughter was now supporting herself and her mother. This situation alone was a wake-up call for the young journalist, and it shook her up. In looking ahead she then realized that if her steady paycheck stopped, she had a total of about $7,000 to fall back on. She was suddenly propelled into action.

As I said in the introduction of this book, the "how-to" of investing – how to buy and sell stocks, how to manage a rental property or how to analyze a business investment – is the same for men as it is for women. However, the reasons *why* women must become investors is very different between the sexes.

We know that we lead very different lives than our mothers did but you may be surprised at just how different. Here are six sound reasons why women need to get into this game called investing.

1) The Statistics

The statistics about women and money are very startling. The following are U.S. statistics, yet I find that for other countries throughout the world these statistics are either very similar or are trending in the same direction.

In the U.S.:

- 47% of women over the age of 50 are single. (This means they are financially responsible for themselves.)

- Women's retirement income is less than that of men because a woman is away from the work force an average of 14.7 years as compared to 1.6 years for men. (Women are typically the primary caretaker of the home.) This, along with lower salaries, adds up to retirement benefits that are only about 1/4 of those of men. (National Center for Women and Retirement Research – NCWRR)

- 50% of marriages end in divorce.
  (And who typically ends up with the children? The woman. So now she is solely financially responsible for herself – and her children.)
  (And what is the #1 subject couples fight about? Money.)

- In the first year after a divorce a woman's standard of living drops an average of 73%.

- As of 2000, women are expected to live an average of 7 to 10 years longer than men, (Ann Letteeresee June 12, 2000), which means they must provide for those extra years. However, married baby boomer women can expect to outlive their husbands by 15 to 20 years on average.

- The average female born between 1948 and 1964 may likely remain in the workforce until at least 74 years of age due to inadequate financial savings and pension coverage. (National Center for Women and Retirement Research, 1996)

- Of the elderly living in poverty:
  - 3 out of 4 are women (Morningstar Fund Investor)
  - 80% of the women were not poor when their husbands were alive.
- Approximately 7 out of 10 women will at some time live in poverty.

What are these statistics telling us? They tell us that more and more women, especially as they become older, are not educated or prepared to take care of themselves financially. We've spent our entire lives taking care of our families but have no ability to care for ourselves in this vital way. We are either depending upon someone else to do it for us – a husband or partner, a boss, a family member, or the government. Or we just figure that it will all work out. The fairy tales we grew up with were just that.

Three final statistics to consider:
1) 90% of all women will have sole responsibility for their finances within their lifetimes… yet 79% of all women have not planned for this.

2) 58% of female baby boomers have less than $10,000 in retirement.

3) It's estimated that only 20% of baby boomer women will be financially secure in their retirement. (*Ms. Magazine*, 2002)

(This means that 80% of us will not be. However, the fact that you are reading this book says that you're leaning toward that 20%. Ideally as more women get on board with investing that 20% will increase significantly.)

2) Avoiding Dependency

You don't go into a marriage expecting a divorce. You don't begin a new job expecting to be laid off. But it happens, and today with more and more frequency. I've said this before, but, women, if you are depending on a husband, a boss, or anyone else for your financial future, think twice. They simply may not be there. Too often we may not even realize just how dependent we are until we're faced with our own personal wake-up call.

Here is my personal story. Robert and I have been business partners since one month after our first date. We've built several businesses over the years.

We were about six years into our entrepreneurial education company when an argument led me to an epiphany. The company was operating in Australia, New Zealand, the U.S., Hong Kong, Singapore, Malaysia, and Canada. We built the businesses with Robert as the figurehead, the spokesperson, the visionary, which made perfect business sense. One day Robert and I had a disagreement. The disagreement grew into a great big fight. In the heat of the argument I stormed out the door of our house. Neither of us were rational at that point. I needed some time to think and headed for a hike in the mountain preserve near our home. As I was alone in my thoughts, reality struck.

All my life I prided myself on being independent. From the time I got my first job in high school I knew that I would not be dependent as long as I could make money. And even though I built this company with Robert from the ground up the truth slapped me in the face. All of the sudden I realized that if Robert and I were to split up then I would not only lose my marriage but I would lose my business! Because Robert was the figurehead of our company, if he left, then the business would collapse. And if he stayed, then I would leave. Either way, the reality was, without ever realizing it, I had set myself up to be totally dependent on Robert. I could not believe it! I know Robert didn't see it that way, but I did. That was my wake-up call. And now I wanted to be sure that whatever decisions I made were decisions that were right for me… and not my bank account.

Robert and I worked through our argument, and it was very clear to both of us that we wanted to be together for a long time. But that wake-up call had a life-changing impact on me. Up to that point I had purchased a few rental properties, but I looked at it as a hobby. Now I saw it as my means to freedom. That's when the passion kicked in and investing was no longer a hobby to me, it was a mission.

There was one huge unexpected benefit that I got as I turned into an investor. Once I understood the game of investing and I learned how to make money passively, without working, then I realized for the first time that I no longer needed Robert. What was even more enlightening was that I discovered that I wanted to be with Robert, not out of need but out of want. At that point our relationship took on a new meaning. We were together simply because we both wanted to be together.

Another immense gift I received is that my self-esteem grew in this whole process. As a result of that, Robert and I had more respect, more love, more equality, and more happiness in our marriage than ever before.

3) No Glass Ceiling

One obstacle for many women in the corporate world is the glass ceiling myth. The glass ceiling professes that because of our gender, women can only move so far up the corporate ladder.

In the world of investing the markets don't care if you're female or male, black or white, a college grad or a high school dropout. The markets only care about how smart you are with your money. The key is education and experience. The smarter you are with your investment choices the greater your success as an investor. There are no limits, no ceilings, glass or otherwise, for women in the world of investing.

4) No Limits on Income

Because of the glass ceiling and because of the still-present wage inequality between men and women, a woman is often limited in the amount of income she can make. Studies show that women, with the same education and experience as their male counterparts earn about 74 cents for every dollar their male peers earn. In investing, the money you can make is unlimited. You are completely responsible for and in control of the amount of money you make as an investor.

Since I didn't want anyone telling me how much money I could make, having no limits on my income appealed to me greatly.

5) Increased Self-Esteem

Personally, I think this is one of the greatest benefits to women investors. It's not unusual for a woman's self esteem to be linked to her ability to provide for herself. Being dependent on anyone for your financial life can lead to a reduced sense of self-worth. You may do things you otherwise would not do if money were no issue.

I've seen women's self-esteem soar once they know how to make it on their own financially. And when a woman's self-esteem rises, then the relationships around her tend to improve. Her life improves overall because she feels good about herself, and she is making choices that are genuinely true to her. With every little victory you accomplish, your confidence increases. Increased confidence leads to higher self-esteem. Higher self-esteem leads to

greater success, which ultimately leads to the greatest gift of all –
freedom.

6) Control of Your Time

One big impediment women have (often more so than men) when
it comes to investing is *time*. This is especially true for mothers
who often spend many waking hours taking care of the children. I
hear from many women, "After I come home from work, I have to
get dinner ready, help my kids with their homework, and clean up
the dishes. By the time everyone's in bed and I have a free moment
to myself I'm exhausted!"

As an investor you are in control of your time. Investing is
something you can do part time or full time. It is something you
can do from home, from the office, anywhere.

It is also something in which you can include your children. Many
mothers have told me that they take their children to look at
properties or potential business investments. And a big plus is that
when you include your children in the investment process you are
actually teaching them to be investors as well. You become a
teacher just like Robert's Rich Dad was to him.

I do not have children, but I certainly understand the desire to
spend time with one's kids. To watch them grow. To be there for all
their "firsts." That's one of the best freedoms of all – time. Being an
investor allows you to spend your time how you want – whether
it's with your children, with your spouse/partner, on vacation, or
looking at potential deals. You are in control of your time.

Summary

These six reasons support why women and investing go hand-in-
hand. The statistics prove how much times have changed for
women and point out that our need for real-life financial education
is no longer a luxury, it's a necessity. Depending on someone else
for your financial future is like rolling the dice in Las Vegas these
days. The reward may be there in the end but the risk is steep.

Glass ceilings and limits to income are what so many women have been fighting against for ages. Both disappear in the world of investing. And then two of the greatest gifts of all – a higher sense of self-worth and time to spend exactly as you want – can be yours. Today, investing is no longer just a good idea for women. It is a must-have.

Chapter Six

"I DON'T HAVE THE TIME!"

*"I believe that we are solely responsible for our choices, and we have
to accept the consequences of every deed, word, and thought
throughout our lifetime."*

– Elizabeth Kubler-Ross

Pat spoke first, "This is all pretty eye-opening. I can certainly relate to feeling dependent on my husband financially. I'm never really comfortable making financial decisions without him because I feel like he makes the money, so I don't have as much input. I have my own little nest-egg that I've put aside that I use for whatever I want.

"What astounds me though and really hits home is my good friend who is in the middle of a divorce after 22 years of marriage. She's going to be left with almost nothing when all is said and done – except for child support. She fits right into those statistics. Plus she hasn't been in the workforce for the past 18 years. She'll be almost 50 and in between trying to figure out how to make ends meet, she's struggling with what to put on her résumé. She's terrified," Pat concluded.

Janice looked a bit uneasy. "Let me ask you this," she began. "I love my business, and I plan to spend the rest of my career in my business or eventually sell the business for a nice profit. Why do I need to invest? I feel like I have a solid plan in place."

"You have a great plan," I told her. "What I'm talking about is having choices. If your plan works out as you envision, then that is wonderful. And knowing you, you'll make it happen. I know for The Rich Dad Company, coming into it at the start financially independent truly escalated our business' success. When we started the company,

Robert and I did not need the money from our company to live on. The same was true for our partner Sharon. So with every decision we made we asked ourselves, 'What is the best decision for the company?' not 'What will put the most money in our pockets?' That alone accelerated the growth of our company tremendously. It led to us making better choices for our business.

"Here's another example of a woman who loves her work," I continued. "I have a very good friend, Carol, who is a dentist. She owns her own practice. Recently she was diagnosed with breast cancer. Thank goodness the doctor caught it early, and she is fine. She called me shortly after the whole ordeal and said, 'This has been a huge wake-up call for me. Here I am a successful dentist, making a great income, loving what I do, and all of a sudden I have cancer. I immediately started to think about what would happen if I couldn't work. My nice secure income would quickly go to zero. And my savings *might* sustain me for one year. It was a scary time. Not only was I facing cancer but on top of it facing a possible financial disaster.'

"As a result of Carol's wake-up call, today she owns several rental properties throwing off a healthy monthly income, and she is setting up her practice to run without her if she ever chooses to leave it.

"Again," I ended, "it's simply about giving yourself choices."

Janice was nodding in agreement.

The #1 Excuse Of Women

"But, Janice, you asked the first, most important question a woman, or anyone for that matter, needs to ask when it comes to starting something new, such as investing. "

"What did I ask?"

"Something that if you don't answer honestly will ruin your chances of success," I said. "First, let me say this: I'm not here today to talk you all into becoming fabulous investors… even though I think that would be a pretty smart thing to do on your part. We're here today to catch up with one another, have a wonderful lunch together, talk about 'the old days,' and enjoy the day."

"That's OK," Pat said. "This is getting kind of good."

"Good, because sometimes I just can't help sharing what I've learned over the years with people I care about. Once I get started it's hard to shut me up. So if I sound like I'm preaching, I apologize. What I've done and what I've learned is not because I'm smart, I have a college degree, I have special skills, or I know more than anyone else. What I've done isn't because I have these brilliant ideas that pop into my head. It has nothing to do with any of that. I've learned from many great teachers – most don't even realize they were teachers. They are business people, investors, writers, parents, and friends. So when I talk about investing and what I'm doing, what I'm sharing with you is a combination of the knowledge and experience of all these people.

"I'm truly not here to talk you into anything. I'm just a bit enthusiastic because I've seen so many women's lives turn around for the better once they got into this game. Instead of me ranting and raving on, if you want to talk further we can do that at another time, but for now let's celebrate our reunion."

What's The Question?

"Not so fast," Janice broke in. "You said I asked an important question. I want to know what I asked."

I looked at Pat and Leslie. "Do you two want to hear this? I can talk with Janice later about it."

"No, go on," Leslie exclaimed. "I definitely want to hear this. I'm just amazed at what I'm hearing because, to be perfectly honest, I've been searching for some answers right along these lines."

Pat added, "You've got my attention, even though some of it hits a little too close to home for me. Go on."

"OK," I started. "Janice did ask the all-important question. But before I get to the question let me give you some lead up to it. Let me ask you all a question. If I said let's all spend three full days a week, every week, working out and getting in shape, what would you say?"

"I'm too busy. I can't leave my business alone that often," Janice started.

"Yeah, I can't take three days a week from my job. That's too much time," Leslie seconded.

"I would if I had the time. I'm really out of shape," Pat finished up.

"Time. It's all about time, isn't it?" I asked. They all nodded. "We're too busy. We don't have the time. Even though it's something that we know would be good for us, the time requirements are too great."

"So what are you getting at?" asked Leslie

I went on, "We often use excuses, disguised as reasons, when we don't want to do something. The reasons sound perfectly rational and acceptable, but in reality it's a person's way of saying, 'I'm not going to do that,' or 'I don't want to do that.' And the number one excuse, or reason, people use today is what?"

"I don't have the time!" Leslie said.

"Exactly! And often we don't have the time. No doubt we're all very busy. How often do we say, 'If there were only more hours in the day.' It's especially true for women. How many of us have full-time careers, kids, a husband or relationship, plus all the additional day-to-day activities. So when someone suggests adding another activity that will demand our time we're ready to explode.

What I've done and what I've learned is not because I'm smart, I have a college degree, I have special skills, or I know more than anyone else.

What I've done isn't because I have these brilliant ideas that pop into my head. It has nothing to do with any of that.

I've learned from many great teachers – most don't even realize they were teachers. They are business people, investors, writers, parents, and friends.

"When we say 'I don't have the time,' we're just saying, 'What I have currently on my plate is more important than the additional activity you're suggesting.' It's not right or wrong to say 'I have no time.' But the question to ask yourself is, 'What truly is most important?' Too often the excuse of no time is an automatic response because we're already overwhelmed and can't possibly imagine adding one more thing to our workload."

"So what if we actually are up to

our eyeballs in work and activities and simply do not have the time?" asked Janice.

"That's a good question," I acknowledged.

"I'm good with the questions, not so good with the answers." Janice laughed.

"Which is a perfect lead-in to your original question," I countered. "The number one reason or excuse I hear from women when I talk to them about getting started in investing is, you guessed it, 'I don't have the time!' So if you are juggling family, career, charities, sports, activities, not to mention just keeping up with friends and everyday life, how do you find the time?

"Unfortunately we cannot add more hours to the day. From talking with many women it seems clear that the way you 'find the time' is to answer Janice's original question."

"Which is?" Janice pleaded.

"The critical question you asked was, 'Why do I need to invest?'"

All three women were now totally bewildered.

"And why is that the most important question?" Leslie asked with a puzzled look on her face.

Your Personal Reason Why

"Because most people think the first step to investing is learning the how-to's," I replied. "How to find a good real estate broker. How to buy a call option. How to spot a good business in which to invest. The how-to's are not difficult to learn. It takes some time (there's that word again) and some education. But the real first step when it comes to investing is to find out why you want or need to invest. Why would you take on this challenge? What will truly motivate and drive you to spend the time and effort to become a good investor?"

"I just want to make enough money so I don't have to go to work every day," Leslie volunteered.

"Will 'making enough money so you don't have to go to work' inspire you to read books, do the leg-work, attend seminars, seek out and meet with investing experts, or give up your days off?" I asked.

"Whew! That sounds like too much work. I get tired just thinking about it," she responded.

"Then that is not your why. If it doesn't inspire you, then it's not a strong and compelling reason to do it," I explained.

"So what is a compelling reason why? Can you give us an example?" asked Pat.

I thought for a moment. "OK. Remember when I asked you about spending three full days a week exercising?" They all shook their heads yes. "Obviously none of you had a compelling reason why you'd want to do that. Each of you came up with a reason why not, why you couldn't fulfill that commitment. Agreed?" I asked.

Again they nodded.

I kept on. "What if you went to your doctor for a check-up and she told you that you had a rare disease, and if you did not work out three full days a week then you would die. Would you now have a compelling reason to work out?"

They were wide-eyed.

"That would certainly do it for me," Janice said. "All of a sudden working out would become my number one priority."

"You've got it!" I said excitedly. "Working out initially had zero priority in your life. Once you discover that reason why it becomes a top priority. That's exactly what I mean when I talk about finding your own personal reason why."

"So if you don't discover the real reason why, then it's not a priority and you probably won't do it," Pat said.

"Or stick with it. If you do start, chances are you'll lose interest and give up," I added. "How many times have we started something that seemed so important but never finished it? It's probably because it sounded like a great idea, but we never took the time to uncover our true reason for doing it. When it comes to starting out in investing there is a big learning curve so it's not enough to say my reason why is 'I want to make more money' or 'I want to buy rental property' or 'I want to retire.' All of those are reasons, but I doubt they would inspire you when you're ready to quit because it gets a little tough or you feel you've done 'enough' and the results aren't there yet. Your personal reason why has to be dazzling and moving so that when you begin to doubt what you're doing ,your why keeps you going."

"So just saying to myself, 'I *should* invest,' or 'So-and-so said it was a good idea,' isn't going to motivate me to keep going because I haven't discovered my deep-seated benefit, what's truly in it for me," Leslie said.

A Few Reasons Why

"Exactly. I heard a fantastic *reason why* the other day," I said. "I was talking with this gentleman, Peter. He is a single dad with a 7-year-old son. He told me, 'I'm an engineer. I see my son for a few minutes in the morning, then he gets picked up for school by one of the other child's parents, and I go off to work. If I'm lucky I get home before he goes to bed. The reason I wanted to become financially free was very simply so that I could drive my son to school every day. That was it. Well, it took me four years and today I am free. The cash flow from my investments pays for my lifestyle. And today I drive my son to school every day. I'm probably the only person on the L.A. freeway stuck in the middle of rush-hour traffic with a huge smile on my face.' Now that is a valuable *reason why*."

"That reminds me of my next-door neighbor," Leslie said. "She and I talk quite often, and she shared with me what frustrated her most about being a single mom. Her parents divorced when she was five, and her father got custody of her. The problem was that her father was never around. He was always working or chasing after his next ex-girlfriend. My neighbor said she had little-to-no guidance or stability growing up. She was basically raised by a series of babysitters. As a result all she wanted was for her own children to know that they were loved, protected, and cared for every day. She just wants to spend as much time with them as possible. Her dilemma, like so many other women, is that she has to work full-time to support her family, which sometimes include nights as well as days. She has her *reason why*. She just has no clue what to do about it. "

"My sister is another example," Pat announced. "Ever since she could open a book she dreamed of traveling the world. She would devour books about foreign lands. Her term papers always took place in exotic locations. She had a huge collection of brochures and articles of all the places she dreamed of visiting. She constantly tells me that she wants to live her dream before she gets too old to enjoy it. She would be very excited by this conversation we're having."

"There are countless *reasons why*. I'm sure everyone has one. We just don't take the time to uncover it. Unfortunately for many of us, our reason why slaps us in the face as a wake-up call."

"What do you mean a 'wake-up call'? asked Janice.

"Remember I mentioned my girlfriend, the dentist? Her *reason why*, became crystal clear when she was diagnosed with cancer. She actually had two wake-up calls. The first was obviously about her health. She started studying up on cancer. What were the possible causes? What could she do differently to better her odds? Did she need to change her diet or her work habits? All of a sudden her health was number one.

"Her second wake-up call concerned money. She realized if she couldn't work, then she had no income coming in. Her savings were almost nonexistent. She had no means of support if she couldn't work. That was the kick in the pants she needed to start taking control of her long-term finances."

"I've seen that often with people when it comes to their health," Janice added. "Most of us never make our health our number-one priority until we're faced with a health problem – it's that first health scare. For me it's always a battle when that alarm clock goes off in the morning – do I go to the gym or turn over and go back to bed?"

"I've done that one a few times," Leslie moaned.

"I've been guilty of that, well, more than a few times," I added. "So going back to that number-one excuse of 'I don't have the time' once you uncover your true *reason why* you want to invest – or your real *reason why* you want to take on anything new – then the excuse disappears."

"Because it becomes a top priority in your life," Pat finished the thought. "Because I can see what's really in it for me."

Leslie jumped in. "It's really no different than when we were all starting out 20 years ago. Our priority then was our career. That's where our focus was. We were excited to take on the challenge! That's where we spent most of our time… in between boys, the beach, and dates… it was number one for each of us. And it happened for each of us. But later it seems like instead of deliberately making things in my life a priority, I *reacted* to what was happening in my life, and that dictated how my life has run so far. I'm just now realizing I never made my priorities a priority."

"That's quite philosophical," Janice kidded. "But truthfully this is a great discussion. What I'm realizing is that I've really given myself only one choice in terms of my future – build my business and sell it – and if it works, great. But what if something unexpected happens, or I get burned out on it? I do need to have more than one option, and I especially like the idea of having money coming in every month without me working for it. Tell me more about that, because it's a subject I know absolutely nothing about. I'm also going to start thinking about my *reason why* I'm going to commit the time and energy into becoming, as you say, financially independent… regardless of what I do with my business. What a freeing idea!"

"What I'm getting out of all of this," Pat added, "is that I'm not sure I've ever stopped to think about what my *reason why* is for anything I do. I just do it because it needs to be done. I've never sat down and said, 'These are my priorities.' I just roll with life day-in and day-out, not questioning *why* I'm doing it. Wow, I can see how this would give me so much more control over my life."

Leslie loudly questioned, "How in the world did we get into such a heavy discussion? Whew! This started out as a nice leisurely lunch, and now we're talking about changing our worlds! Who started this whole thing anyway?" We were all silent for the moment. Then she finished, "Well whoever did… thanks… it's just what I needed to hear."

We all agreed to keep in touch with each other. Maybe we could track down Martha and Tracey next time. It was a fabulous reunion. We were so glad we all made the effort to get together. We applauded Pat one last time for organizing the lunch, and we stepped outside into the brisk air to catch our cabs. As the first cab approached, Janice yelled, "Oh no! I was supposed to be at this grand opening a half an hour ago! I lost track of all time!" As she jumped into the cab, she said, "This was too much fun! Call me!" And she was off in a flurry.

The three of us looked at each other – yep, some things never change.

How To Discover Your Personal Reason Why
For Becoming Financially Independent

Find a quiet place with no distractions – a setting that allows you to get in touch with yourself. Take your time with this process. Don't rush through it. Your personal reason why may come to you in an instant or you may find you want to think about it over time.

1   a) Ask yourself, "What is my true reason for wanting to be financially independent?"
Think about:
    • *What you would do if you never had to work again.*

    • *What if you had all the time in the world to spend exactly as you wanted?*

    • *How would your life be different if money were not a worry?*

    b) Write down everything that comes up.

2   a) Ask yourself again, "What is my deep-down core reason for wanting to be financially independent?" Look deeper.
    b) Write down everything that comes up.

3   a) Ask yourself again, going deeper, "What is my innermost, heartfelt reason for wanting to be financially independent?"
    b) Write down everything that comes up.

Continue to ask yourself the question again and again, going deeper within yourself each time, until your personal reason why is crystal clear.

Chapter Seven

WHAT DOES IT MEAN TO BE FINANCIALLY INDEPENDENT?

"I do not wish (women) to have power over men; but over themselves."

– Mary Wollstonecraft

What exactly is *financial independence?* Does it mean you have a high-paying job and you can support yourself? Does it mean you've saved up a lump sum of money to last you the next 30 or 40 years? Is it based on a much-anticipated inheritance? Or even alimony? For many people financial freedom translates to: "I'm going to work until I'm 65 and then retire."

There are a lot of ideas out there on what constitutes financial independence. The following is the definition I've been using for many years and the meaning of which allowed me to retire at age 37.

First, let me say this: I highly recommend you read *Rich Dad Poor Dad*. *Rich Dad Poor Dad* was written by my husband, Robert. It is a true story based upon his two "fathers." His "Poor Dad" was his biological father – a highly educated PhD. and superintendent of schools for the state of Hawaii. Robert calls him his "Poor Dad" because no matter how much money he made he was always broke at the end of every month. Robert's "Rich Dad," as I told my friends, was his best friend's father. He had very little education and went on to build a real estate empire in Hawaii. So *Rich Dad Poor Dad* is a simple story about what two fathers teach their sons – Robert and his best friend – about the subject of money.

Most of the philosophy and concepts around money, wealth, and financial freedom that I follow are a result of what I've learned from Robert speaking and writing about his Rich Dad. So instead of giving you a third-hand version of the Rich Dad lessons, I propose you read *Rich Dad Poor Dad*. It will give you the fundamentals and a strong foundation upon which to build. This is truly a must-read if you are serious about your financial future.

The most surprising thing I discovered from the Rich Dad information is that what Rich Dad did to acquire his wealth is almost 180 degrees opposite of what we are all told by the "financial experts." It is also not rocket science. It's not complicated. It simply takes some time, education, and common sense.

So getting back to *financial independence*, what is it? Let me clearly state that the following is the definition and formula I followed and continue to follow to sustain and grow my financial sovereignty. I've heard financial independence defined in many ways by many people. There is no right or wrong answer. I am simply explaining the terms and criteria I use in investing that led me to become financially free.

The formula I use to obtain financial independence is the formula that Robert's Rich Dad taught him. Again, for a more thorough explanation please read *Rich Dad Poor Dad*.

The formula is this:

> I buy and create assets that generate cash flow. The cash flow from my assets pay for my living expenses. Once my monthly cash flow from my assets is equal to or greater than my monthly living expenses then I am financially independent. I am financially free because my assets are throwing off cash flow and are working for me. I no longer have to work for money.

What Is An Asset?

Robert's Rich Dad had a way of putting things in very simplistic terms. His definition of an asset that I use is:

"An asset, if you stop working, is something that puts money in your pocket." Period. Simple. If you stopped working today, meaning your salary stopped, from where would money flow into your pocket?

Most women who I explain this to for the first time reply, "Nowhere." There'd be no money.

One woman with whom I spoke insisted, "But my diamond bracelet is an asset."

To which I responded, "Are you going to sell it?"

"Of course not!" she said indignantly.

"Well then is it putting money in your pocket today?"

"No," she admitted quietly.

"Then it's simple. According to Rich Dad's definition it's not an asset. The day you sell it and it puts money in your pocket, then it will be considered an asset."

An asset may be a rental property that has a positive cash flow. It may be a business in which you invested that gives you a cash flow every year. It could be a stock that pays a dividend. The key is that it is an investment from which you receive money on a regular basis – it provides positive cash flow.

On the flip side, a liability, according to Rich Dad, is something that takes money from your pocket. So if you stopped working, chances are your car would take money from your pocket each month through car payments, gasoline, and maintenance. Your house would take money from you each month in the form of a mortgage payment, property taxes, insurance, and upkeep. These all provide negative cash flow.

According to Rich Dad the reason people get into trouble financially or never get ahead is because they have liabilities that they have been led to believe are assets. One of the most important lessons I learned from Rich Dad was to know the difference between an asset and a liability.

So the first part of the formula is to buy or create assets. And an asset, according to Rich Dad, throws off positive cash flow.

What Is Cash Flow?

There are two key items I focus on when acquiring assets. My first and primary focus is cash flow.

Let's say you put so much money into an investment. It may be stocks, real estate, or investing in a business venture. Every month (quarter or year) you receive a return (or payment to you) on the money you invested.

In the world of stocks a dividend from a stock you purchase is a form of cash flow.

Here's an example from the world of business: you invest $25,000 in your friend's new gourmet food business. (Not that I necessarily recommend investing your money with friends… that's another story.) Each month you receive a check from the profits for $400. That $400 you get each month is cash flow.

Here's an example from the world of real estate: you pay $20,000 as a down payment for a $100,000 two-unit rental property. At the end of each month, after collecting the rent, paying the expenses of the property, and paying the mortgage, your net profit is $300. That $300 is your cash flow, and it flows right to your pocket.

Why else would you invest, if not for cash flow?

Most people invest for one of two reasons – *cash flow* or *capital gains.*

Capital Gains

Capital gains is a one-time profit. Cash flow is ongoing profit. For example, you buy a house for $100,000. You sell it for $130,000. After paying a commission to the real-estate agent and closing costs, your net profit is $20,000. That $20,000 is your capital gain.

If you buy a stock at $20 per share and sell it at $25 per share, then the profit you made from the sale is considered capital gain.

In order to realize capital gains you must sell your investment or asset. To get further capital gains, or profits, you then must buy and sell the next investment or asset.

Cash flow continues to flow in as long as you own the asset (and it is managed well). Once you sell that asset then the cash flow ends. Once you sell the investment your profits would then fall under the category of capital gains.

How Do You Compute Cash Flow?

Computing your cash flow from stock dividends and businesses (assuming you are strictly an investor in the business and not actually operating the business) is pretty straightforward. When you purchase a stock that pays a dividend, that dividend is your cash flow. There is really nothing to calculate regarding cash flow. But there is another important formula to calculate, along with cash flow, which we'll talk about next.

Calculating the cash flow with a pure business investment is no different. You put up so much money as your investment, and you receive a check each month or quarter from that business for the use of your money. The cash flow you receive typically comes from the profits of that business.

If this sounds unfamiliar, it shouldn't be. It's no different than a savings account. The interest you receive on your savings can be considered cash flow. The problem with savings is that with the interest rates currently around one to two percent your cash flow is next to nothing. As an investor you want your money working hard for you. A one to two percent return is very lazy.

With investment real estate, whether it's a single-family house, apartment building, office building, or shopping center, the computation is the same. The equation is:

Rental Income
– Expenses
– Mortgage Payment (Loan)
= CASH FLOW

The essential part of the equation is to have your cash flow be positive, not negative.

Why Is Cash Flow So Important To Financial Independence?

Financial independence means only one thing to me: FREEDOM.

I am free to do what I want, whether it's to have a life of leisure or pursue a new business adventure. I am free to be with the people I choose. I'm free to set the schedule I want. My time is truly my time.

I buy and create assets that generate cash flow. The cash flow from my assets pay for my living expenses.

Once my monthly cash flow from my assets is equal to or greater than my monthly living expenses then I an financially independent.

I am financially free because my assets are throwing off cash flow and are working for me. I no longer have to work for money.

Freedom means that I have more choices. If you had a choice between flying coach or flying first class, which would you choose? Most people don't have that choice. They fly coach because that's all they can afford. If you had a choice between eating at a cheap, good Mexican taco stand or dining at a five-star gourmet restaurant, which would you choose? It depends on what you're in the mood for. (I'd probably opt for the taco stand.) The point is with financial freedom you have that choice. For many people they have only one choice – the cheap meal.

So how does cash flow fit into all of this? As long as I *have* to work, I'm not free. (I may *choose* to work, which is very different from *having* to work.) If I *have* to do something every day to generate money to live on then I am not free.

What I love about positive cash flow is that the money comes in every month whether I work or not. My apartment buildings throw off money every month that goes right to my pocket. My commercial properties generate generous returns that I receive like clockwork every month. Robert's book royalties bring in income every month for which he no longer has to work. He writes the book one time and, if the book has good value and is recommended by people who read it, then the cash flows in. It comes in whether he works or not.

The number-one goal is to get more cash flow coming in than is going out for living expenses. I want to buy and create things that generate that cash flow without me working for it. We call those things assets.

I want my assets working for me, instead of me working for money.

This is why capital gains is a secondary benefit to me, not a primary mission. I have to sell the asset in order to receive the capital gains. That money then gets used up or spent on living expenses and then I have to go find another investment to buy and then sell again. That money is then spent again on living expenses and the cycle continues. I'm never really free.

Others say, "I'll save up enough money to live on for the rest of my life." And that's fine. Just think about this: how long will you have to work and save until you have enough money to live on? What will the interest rate be on your savings when you are in retirement? Are you going to have to watch every penny you spend for fear of running out of money? Will your standard of living have to go down in order to stretch the money you've saved? Just a few questions to think about...

I know that for Robert and me, we had one goal: buy and create assets that generate the cash flow to pay for our living expenses every month. In 1994 we did "retire" by doing just that.

The beauty is that you do not need a huge amount of money to be financially free. In 1994 Robert and I had $10,000 coming in every month from our investments. Our living expenses at the time were about $3,000 a month. At that point we were free. We had more than enough money flowing in every month to handle our living expenses.

Of course we didn't want to stop there, so we continued to buy and create assets. Our cash flow grew, which allowed our living expenses to grow, which elevated our lifestyle.

What Is The Second Thing You Focus On When Analyzing An Asset?

I mentioned earlier that I have two key focuses when looking at a potential investment. The first is cash flow. The second key item I focus on, which goes hand-in-hand with cash flow, is the return on investment or ROI.

What Is A Return On Investment?

Your return on investment is exactly that. It's the amount of cash the money you invested is paying or returning to you. In other words, how hard is the money you invest working for you?

There are several ways to calculate the return on investment depending on what you are measuring. When I refer to return on investment I typically mean what is called a cash-on-cash return on investment. I am interested in only one thing and that's how much cash is flowing into my pocket.

Some formulas take depreciation into account when calculating ROI. Another formula assumes that the cash flow you are receiving is being re-invested immediately and takes that into account. Each formula is accurate, depending on what you want to measure. For me, I like to keep it simple. It's all about the cash flow.

How Do You Calculate Cash-On-Cash Return On Investment?

The calculation is very simple. It is shown as a percentage and usually computed as an annual figure. The equation is:

The Annual Cash Flow /Amount of Cash Invested
= Cash-On-Cash Return On Investment

For example, I'm buying a rental property. The property costs $100,000. I am going to make a down payment of 20% or $20,000, cash. Each month I have a positive cash flow of $200 for an annual cash flow of $2,400. That $2,400 (my annual cash flow) divided by $20,000 (the amount of cash I invested in the property) = 12% cash-on-cash ROI

Let's consider a stock purchase. You buy $2,500 worth of a stock that pays a dividend. You receive an annual dividend of $100. That $100 divided by $2,500 = 4% cash-on-cash ROI.

Now, let's look at the average savings account today. You might receive a 2% interest rate on your savings. Calculating this backward, if you have $1,000 in savings, then the bank will pay you an annual return of $20.

Again, the formula is simple. How much cash am I investing? And how much cash am I receiving from that investment?

The whole reasoning behind focusing on cash flow is that you want your money working hard for you so that you don't have to work hard for your money. The cash-on-cash return on investment measures specifically how hard your money is working for you and lets you compare the performance of your investments apples for apples. If you receive a 2% ROI, then it's not working very hard. If you receive a 50% ROI, then you have a real team member.

Stay Tuned

The path I followed that led me to become financially free is not rocket science. The formula is actually quite *simple*. However, it's not necessarily *easy*. It does take time and education. It will not happen overnight. But I guarantee you that when you start to see your cash flow coming in, the game becomes a lot of fun… and your efforts become well worth the journey.

So if this formula is so simple then what holds women back from taking action and taking control of their financial lives?

We already addressed the number-one excuse women use to not do something – they say, *and believe* – "I don't have the time." I trust it's clearer to you that you can always make the time for something that is important to you.

It's not that we don't have the time, it's that we choose to do other things with our time – granted, most of us are running at a million miles an hour already. Just know that if you're saying to yourself, as you may be right now, "I don't have the time," then you haven't yet made this a priority – you haven't found your *reason why*. But I can tell you first-hand that when women make their financial well-being a priority there is no stopping them. And more and more women are doing just that.

So how else do we women hold ourselves back? The second most popular excuse I hear from the thousands of women I talk to borders not just on silly, but on utter stupidity. Not only is it not a valid excuse it's so far from the truth it's absurd. The number-two excuse we women use is…

Chapter Eight

"I'm Not Smart Enough!"

"I think the key is for women not to set any limits."
– Martina Navratilova

About one week after our New York lunch I was in my car heading to a meeting when my cell phone rang.

"Hi, Kim, this is Leslie. Do you have a minute?"

"Sure."

"I've been thinking a lot about our conversation at lunch, about investing and becoming financially independent, and it all sounds good. It seems to be exactly what I want, but I keep coming back to the same problem again and again."

"What's the problem?" I asked.

Leslie explained, "All my life I've been into art. Into colors, shapes, style, technique. That's how my mind works. My brain doesn't work methodically and analytically. The bottom line is I'm hopeless when it comes to numbers and math. *I just don't think I'm smart enough when it comes to investing.* And every time I start to think about getting started my eyes just glaze over. I even went out and bought The Wall Street Journal. I might as well be reading Chinese! I think there are people who just have a natural knack for this kind of thing and understand the numbers, but it ain't me."

Leslie's frustration was pretty apparent. So I treaded lightly. "First let me ask you this. Have you come up with your reason why you want to start investing?"

"I'm crystal clear on the why," Leslie replied. "I just want to paint. Art is my passion. The problem is I'm so busy working at the gallery so I can pay my bills that I never have time to paint. I want to take my paints and easel and spend my days painting at wonderful and unique locations. Ideally I want to travel to Europe and paint there, as well as study the great masters. There are fabulous art courses available that I would love to take. If I had only one day left to live, I would paint. Yes, I'm well aware of my reason why."

"Congratulations. Now your process begins," I declared.

"What process?" she asked still a bit frustrated.

"Getting rich or becoming financially free is not going to happen overnight. Whenever we're learning something new there is a learning curve we all have to go through. And it can be pretty uncomfortable, especially in the beginning, because we are going into an arena we know very little about."

"I guess it's like when I first learned to drive a car," she said. "I felt like an idiot at first because I'd step on the gas too hard or jump on the brake and nearly go through the windshield. I almost crashed the car my first time on the road."

"That's exactly what I'm talking about. Today you don't think twice about the gas pedal, the brake, or even the steering. It's almost automatic. In the beginning the learning curve was huge. Now it's second nature," I assured her.

"So it's a process, and there is a lot to learn," she went on. "But I just don't know if I'm smart enough to take this on. Investing really seems to be such a man's game. Maybe their knack for numbers is better than mine. I don't know if I can compete in a man's game."

"First of all," I said, "you're right. Men are good with numbers… 38-24-36… to be exact."

Leslie laughed.

"But seriously, why do you think it's a man's game?"

Leslie answered, "Well, I don't see or hear of many women investors in the news. The top investors all seem to be men. I personally don't know of any women role models when it comes to money or investing. I think men have a better understanding of investing than women do."

"A question for you," I said, calmly. "Were men better than women at choosing elected officials? Is that why only men voted years ago? Were men better students than women? Is that why women were barred from universities and colleges? Were men better at hearing and weighing evidence? Is that why for years only men were seated on juries?"

"Of course not!" Leslie exclaimed.

"Understand there's a big difference between doing something better and doing something *longer*," I emphasized.

"In terms of you thinking that you're not smart enough when it comes to investing, there are just three key things you need to understand, and then I bet that thought will vanish forever. It did for me."

"OK, I'm all ears. What are they?" she asked.

Our phone conversation continued, and I told her what I am now telling you.

What We Women Have Been Taught

1) Education

Let's face it, there has not been a lot of good information out there for women when it comes to the subject of money. Actually, much of what is being taught borders on downright demeaning and debilitating – how to balance a checkbook, how to buy car insurance, how to cut down on spending, or how to save pennies at the grocery store. Honestly, I think we're a bit smarter than that.

Yes, you have to get your finances in order. Yes, you absolutely need to know the basics. That's all very important. But my point is that that alone is not enough today. That's just the beginning for laying the foundation. Once you understand the basics, then it's time to take an active role toward attaining your own financial goals.

If I hear a man patronizingly say one more time, "Oh my wife handles all our finances," I will scream. Nine times out of ten she doesn't handle the finances. She pays the bills and balances the checkbook. That's it. If you probe further you find she abdicates all the investing decisions and major buying decisions to her husband. He handles the buying and selling of stocks, the real estate transactions, and most, if not all, of the major financial decisions.

And when her husband passes away and she is left to handle the financial affairs, she has no clue what to do. The alarming fact is that 80 percent of women living in poverty were not poor when their husbands were alive. Remember, 90 percent of us will be solely responsible for our financial affairs at some point in our lives. So a woman's husband is gone, and she has had no experience or education with finances, so she either makes bad decisions or asks "Mr. Helper" – the financial planner, the stockbroker, the real estate broker, the estate planner – to come to her rescue. "I'll take care of that for you," he says. "Let me help you manage your money. I'll set up the perfect investment portfolio for you and you won't even have to think about it." Well, sweetheart, if you are not thinking about your own money, do you really think someone else is?

Here is a scary scenario from Dawn in St. Louis. She writes:

"I'm 58 years old. My husband passed away unexpectedly. I have no idea how much money we have or where it is held, for that matter. He managed the money himself and prided himself in making sure I never worried about money, which means we never talked about the subject.

Now that he's gone I feel like a helpless one-year-old who wants to stand up but just keeps falling down. I've been in the dark all these years. Just before my husband's funeral began I went to my girlfriend and asked, 'How do you pay for a funeral?' I'm completely lost."

So if you are serious about taking control of your finances and you don't want to end up like Dawn, then the bottom line is that it will take time, education, and making more than a few mistakes. It's a process. It won't happen overnight. But please do not make the biggest mistake of all, which is thinking that men know more than you. Just because someone calls himself a "financial expert," don't assume he knows anything about what is best for you and your money. If you think, "They all know more than me." then you will fall prey to the "Mr. Helpers" of the world, and you will never be in control of your money.

Yes, you have to get your finances in order. Yes, you absolutely need to know the basics. That's all very important.

But that alone is not enough today. That's just the beginning… the foundation.

Once you understand the basics, it's time to take an active role toward attaining your own financial goals.

The first step is to start getting educated. What exactly does getting educated mean? There is so much information out there; where do you begin?

The exact starting point will be different for everyone. You may start by learning about the different types of investments available. You will probably find that you are attracted to a certain type of investment. For me, it is investment real estate. For my girlfriend the accountant it is stock options. My friend the entrepreneur loves to invest in start-up companies. Through the process of getting educated you'll discover which type of investment suits you best.

Here is a partial list of resources to help you get the education you need:

- **Read books.**
  There are hundreds of books about money and investing for those of you who are just getting started and for those who are seasoned investors. There is a glossary of recommended reading in the back of this book.

- **Listen to Audiotapes and CDs.**
  Keep them in your car and listen to them as you drive. Take advantage of the time you have sitting in traffic, commuting to and from work, or running errands. The audiotapes and CDs may range in subject from money management and investing to personal development. Your attitude and mindset plays a crucial role in your success with anything you take on. As Henry Ford said, "If you think you can do a thing or think you can't do a thing, you're right." A few recommended CDs are listed in the glossary.

- **Invest in educational seminars, workshops, and conferences.**
  These may be free programs in your area or classes you pay to attend. Various community colleges, businesses, community clubs and organizations, and local investment groups often offer such programs. Some programs are geared directly for women.

- **Read financial newspapers and magazines.**
  The Wall Street Journal, Investor's Business Daily, and *Barron's* are three newspapers heaped with investment information. Even if you don't understand all the terminology, keep reading and your knowledge will dramatically increase over time. There is an excellent book put out by *The Wall Street Journal* called *Guide To Understanding Money and Investing*. This book teaches you how to read and interpret The Wall Street Journal.

- **Subscribe to your local business journal newspaper.**
  Here you will get a wealth of information about what is happening in your area. You will quickly become aware of the number of articles that relate to or affect various investment decisions.

- **Talk with real estate, stock and business brokers.**
  Ask them questions. They can give you a wealth of information. Just be aware that most are there to sell you

something, so keep your eyes open. I have found that the most successful brokers are the ones very willing to share information and education with others.

Three tips: 1) There are just as many, maybe more, bad brokers than there are good brokers. To find a reputable and knowledgeable broker ask around for referrals. **2)** Specifically with real estate brokers, be sure you are working with an investment real estate broker and not a residential broker who simply wants to sell you a house in which to live. The two do not speak the same language. **3)** Whenever possible, work with brokers who are actual investors. Many brokers are merely salespeople, not investors. A broker who is also an investor understands your needs and wants much better than a broker who is not.

- **Talk with other investors.**
  Seek out people who are investing in what you are interested in and talk with them. Again, you'll probably find that the more successful investors are happy to share what they know with you.

- **Join a women's investment club.**
  According to Ken Janke of Better Investing, women now account for the majority of stock market investment clubs. "In 1960, investment club membership was 90 percent male, 10 percent female. Today it's over 60 percent female." Personally, I recommend clubs that focus on investment *education*. I am not necessarily a supporter of clubs whose members pool their money to buy investments. I've seen several friendships sour because of unclear rules around their joint investments. To find women's investment clubs look in your local newspapers and magazines for such meetings happening around town. Go online and search for specific women's clubs in your area. Attend your local businesswomen's network meetings and ask for referrals to investment clubs.

- **Start your own women's investment club.**
  Hold your standards high. Accept only women who are serious about their financial future and who will support and encourage one another to go for their goals.

  What do you do at an investment club?

  – It can begin as a study group where you read and discuss a book as a group. Or choose an audio/video product to study together. (There is a list of Rich Dad products in the back of the book which can be a good starting point for a new or existing club.)

  – Bring in guest speakers such as successful investors, knowledgeable brokers (who are there to educate, not sell you a product), property managers, sales experts (knowing how to sell will assist you in almost anything you undertake) – anyone who will add to your knowledge of investing.

  – Learn how to analyze potential investments. Bring specific real estate deals, possible stock trades, and business investments to the group that the women can analyze and learn from together. Find an experienced investor or professional in the beginning who will walk through the basics of how to analyze these investments. The more investments you look at the better your ability becomes to know a good opportunity from a bad opportunity.

- **Join a CASHFLOW Club in your area.**
  There are almost 2,000 CASHFLOW Clubs throughout the world. Go online to find the club closest to you. You can also visit our Web site at www.richdad.com for a listing of CASHFLOW Clubs. Each CASHFLOW Club is different. Most clubs play the CASHFLOW board game on a regular basis, support one another with their investment goals, bring in guest speakers, and, most importantly, learn together how to make the most of their financial futures.

- **Use the Internet.**
  Go online and seek out all sorts of information about the investments of your choice. The Web is an incredible source of quick reference materials, meetings and conferences, contacts, investment Web sites with chat rooms, and discussion forums.

- **Drive around town.**
  Get a feel for what is happening with real estate and businesses in your own backyard. Often people think they have to find the "right" city or market in which to invest when in reality they can usually find incredible opportunities right around the corner from their houses. The closer you are physically to your investments the better your probability of success. It's much easier to keep your finger on the pulse of a market if it's two blocks away versus 2,000 miles away.

- **Watch the financial news programs on TV.**
  Again, you may not comprehend it all but you'll certainly learn a lot, and you'll hear the vocabulary of the investment world. The more you listen, the more you'll understand.

- **Subscribe to financial newsletters.**
  Newsletters can give you a quick summary of what is happening in the various investment markets, economic trends both regionally and globally, and insights into what to watch for in the future. Several are listed in the glossary.

- **Ask questions. Ask questions. Ask questions.**
  Remember, women, we have the advantage here. Since we've had so little investment education we don't have to pretend to know all the answers. The more questions you ask, the smarter you become.

Plus, you may find a new mentor in the process.

By the way, the education never stops. As long as you want to keep growing your investments and expanding your portfolio there are always new levels of learning. As the markets change and my investments grow I find I have to keep updating and expanding my financial knowledge.

2) The Process Versus The Outcome

I always remind myself that investing is a process. There is no secret formula. There is no get-rich-quick pill you can take. You don't go to bed one night and wake up wealthy in the morning. There may be people out there who promise these things but I have yet to see one that lasts for the long-term.

It's no different than losing weight. If you want to lose weight and keep it off, then there is a process you go through. You exercise regularly. You make some changes to your diet. And over time you start to see the results. It doesn't happen overnight… unless you have liposuction. But even then you still have to adjust your lifestyle to make it last.

In the process of becoming investors, we learn. We get some hands-on experience. We make mistakes. We learn from our mistakes. We get more experience. And in this process our knowledge, our confidence, and our abilities grow. Not to mention our bank accounts. But the key is this – *this process we go through is even more important than the end goal itself.* Because who we become in the process, as a result of all the learning, mistakes, and experiences, is where the real value lies. There is a Chinese proverb that says,

The journey is the reward.

In 1985 when Robert and I went through our "year from hell" it was undeniably the worst year of our lives. My self-esteem was crushed. The upsets were constant. My inner voice, what I was saying to myself, was persistently negative; "You can't do that." "You're going to fail." "You don't know anything." "You're hopeless." I would honestly go to bed some nights thinking how much easier it would be if I just never woke up. It was without doubt the lowest point in my life.

And now many years later looking back on that time, I realize that Robert and I were both going through our own processes. There was no pretending; it was miserable. Yet, by going through that process, hitting bottom and then pulling ourselves back up, it was probably one of the best things that could have happened for both of us. When I was in the middle of it all I honestly didn't know if I had it in me to get through it. But by going through that process together, doing what we needed to do individually and as a couple, and coming out the other end successfully, it was an unbelievable character-building experience. As a result, that extremely difficult time made each of us stronger and smarter individually and more committed and assured as a couple. Who I became in the process and who Robert became in the process was invaluable. That was the true reward at the end of the process.

I will guarantee you that in your own process you will make mistakes – sometimes huge mistakes. You will be challenged. You'll have fearful moments. There will be times when you have to make decisions without a clear outcome. It is at these times when our character is tested. If we shy away from the challenge, we don't grow. We don't learn. If we take on the challenge – whether we are successful or not – it is a given that we will grow and expand who we are. And that gain of "intellectual and emotional capital" is priceless.

Chapter Nine

How to Get Smarter...
Quickly

"If I had my life to live again, I'd make the same mistakes, only sooner."

— *Tallulah Bankhead*

The lights went on for Leslie. "It's not that I'm not smart," she started "It's that I've never been taught this stuff. No one has ever taught me to think this way. It's no different than if I took up horseback riding. I'd have to start at the beginning and take it literally step by step."

"That's it."

"I have to tell you though," Leslie confessed. "I have turned on the financial news programs a few times, and I get completely lost in all the terms and vocabulary they use. It completely overwhelms and confuses me. It's hard to follow when I don't know what half of the words mean."

3) Jargon

"You bring up a really good point," I replied. "This is actually point number three. It's called jargon and there is a lot of it in the vocabulary of money and investing."

I went on, "I think much of the confusion around investing has to do with the words the experts, semi-experts, so-called experts, and non-experts use. Sometimes I think people use all that jargon to confuse us on purpose, either to make themselves sound smart or to confuse us into buying something. We don't want to admit we don't know what they're talking about. I've done it. I'll be talking

Words are powerful tools. Master them and your comprehension level of new information increases dramatically. When you come across a word you don't understand... find it in a dictionary, understand what the word means, and then continue reading.

to someone and they'll throw out words I don't know and instead of asking them to explain it I pretend to understand because I don't want to look stupid. Guilty as charged."

"I hate to admit it but I did exactly that two months ago," Leslie said, laughing. "I went to a grand opening of a new Italian restaurant. The owner was a client of mine from the gallery. I joined in on a group discussing the stock market. They were all excited about this new company that just went public. They said they had friends of friends involved in the company and how it was going to be the next Microsoft. Well, talk about jargon! They were bouncing around all this fancy lingo. It was just gibberish to me. I remember something about a price/spending ratio and that the stock traded on the Nestech exchange. They sounded so knowledgeable. and they were so excited. Even though I didn't know what they were talking about I couldn't help but feel like I had some secret information about this stock that no one else had, except for this small group. So the next day I bought some shares. That was two months ago. The stock today is worth half of what I bought it at, and now what I'm hearing is that the future prediction for the company doesn't look too bright."

I laughed. "I think the terms you heard were price/*earnings* ratio, which compares a stock's price to the company's earnings over the past year, and the Nasdaq exchange, which is a completely electronic exchange. They have no physical trading floor.

"But don't feel bad about wanting to get in on the Cinderella stock. We all want to believe the fairy tale, I reassured her. "If it makes you feel any better, I not only believed in the fairy tale, I thought I had bought shares in the actual goose who laid the golden eggs! I bought into a private stock fund. I so wanted to believe all the promises, all the too-good-to-be-true profits to be made. All the excitement, the secret formula, the Holy Grail. Because I didn't understand the words and phrases they were using, I didn't know how to verify what was true and what wasn't. They *sounded* like they knew what they were talking about. So I bought it all. The next thing I knew the company was under investigation and the owner was being hauled off to jail. Even as all the negative publicity surfaced I still believed the headlines were a lie and the promises would come true. It turns out the publicity was true, and I lost my entire investment. The bottom line – I didn't speak the language, and I didn't bother to learn it because I wanted the fairy tale to come true."

Leslie let out a big sigh, "Sorry for your loss... but it does make me feel better to know that no one gets it right every time. It also makes me feel better to know that I'm not the only one who gets confused and overwhelmed with all the financial jargon."

"You'll appreciate this story," I told her. "Robert was doing an interview one morning in New York City at one of the national financial news TV programs. The interviewer used all sorts of jargon – derivatives, P/E ratios, resistance levels, etc. Robert stopped him in the middle of the discussion and said, 'I prefer to keep the language simple.' and Robert continued the interview using common everyday words. As we stepped outside a young man approached. He was about 29, very nicely dressed in a suit and overcoat. He said he worked on Wall Street. And then he shook Robert's hand and said, 'I just watched your interview, and I want to thank you for keeping it simple so everyone can understand what you were saying.' I thought that was quite a compliment coming from someone who worked in the industry."

"Whew! I feel a big relief," Leslie admitted. "I think a lot of women may think they're not smart enough to enter the investment world because, like me, they think they are the only ones who don't understand. I'm really catching on that this is an educational process, and you just keep learning as you go."

She finished with, "Thanks for your time! That clears up quite a bit. When are you next in New York?"

"I'll be there in about two months," I said.

"If you have time, let's get together. Lunch is on me!"

How You Know When You Don't Know

I was taught a valuable tool by a friend of mine who has studied for many years on how people learn. She asked me, "Have you ever found yourself re-reading the same paragraph again and again?"

"Yes." I said. "I do that often. Why is that?" Her research found that when people read and go past a word they do not understand, then they lose focus of what they are reading. This causes them to almost unknowingly re-read the sentence or paragraph several times. Once people read a word they don't know the meaning of, then comprehension of the entire piece they are reading goes down. So I asked my friend, "How do you overcome that?"

"It's easy," she said. "All you have to do is look up the word in the dictionary, understand what the word means, and then continue reading. Your comprehension level increases dramatically."

So now I do my best to keep a dictionary close by and look up words I don't understand. And a sure sign that I've gone past a misunderstood word is when I find myself re-reading a section several times.

When it comes to the world of investing, the jargon is rampant. I may read four words in one sentence that I don't understand. I want to just race past them and pretend they're not important. Instead I do my best to force myself to pick up the dictionary and look up the words. It's more than simply reading the definition. I want to be sure I clearly understand its meaning. Sometimes I revert back to grade school where the teacher would tell me to use the word in a sentence. It works! It can be a bit time-consuming at first but it definitely increases my understanding of what I'm reading, and I increase my vocabulary daily.

The glossary in the back of this book defines many common financial and investment terms. Not every word you'll come across is included, so I've also added some good investment and financial reference books to add to your library and to help you feel more informed when the jargon is flying.

Better Understanding, Better Results

I was talking with an investment real estate broker years ago about a 24-unit apartment building. And he began spouting all the terminology. "The loan-to-value ratio is 80 percent. The cap rate is 9 percent. The internal rate of return is 19 percent." (All these terms are in the glossary.) And on and on he went. So I asked him, "What exactly does a cap rate mean?" He said, "Well the higher the cap rate the better the deal."

"But how exactly do you determine a cap rate? What's the equation? And what specifically does it measure?"

He just looked at me blankly and then said, "It's not really that important; what's important is what a great deal this building is."

The fact is he had no idea what he was talking about. He just used the words but he had no understanding of what the words meant. And you'll appreciate this: not only was this real estate agent baffled by his own jargon but his numbers on this particular property made no sense either. It was not a great deal.

Three Easy Rules

When it comes to jargon, the three rules I've learned to follow are:

1) **Increase your vocabulary every day.**

    Don't be intimidated or, more importantly, lazy, when a word is used you don't understand. If you're having a conversation and an unfamiliar word is used, ask the person who used it what it means or write it down and then later go look it up. If you're reading or watching TV and unknown terminology creeps in, look up the word or words in a dictionary.

2) Ask questions.

Always be curious. Even when you have some knowledge on the subject, keep asking questions. You can always learn more. Two things happen when you ask an expert or semi-expert questions.

a.) You build instant rapport with that person because he or she sees that you are really interested in his or her subject.

b.) You learn more.

3) Look stupid whenever possible.

Don't be afraid to say, "I don't know." The fastest way to impede your learning is to pretend to know all the answers – to act as if you know what someone is talking about when you don't. Being afraid to look stupid only makes you stupid.

I truly think one of the advantages we women have today is that most of us have not been educated in the world of money, finance, and investing. So we're not afraid to say, "I don't know." We haven't been expected to know. We're not afraid to ask questions. We're not afraid to admit the fact that even though we appear to be superwomen ten times over, we actually do not have all the answers.

Do not let the jargon and all those intimidating and confusing words become an obstacle for you. They are only words. And every word has a definition that can be looked up in a dictionary. Instead of being overwhelmed, be excited each time you hear a new financial term because with each new word you learn you become a much smarter and better investor.

Chapter Ten

"I'M SCARED STIFF!"

"You gain strength, courage, and confidence by every experience in which you really stop to look fear in the face. You must do the thing which you think you cannot do."

– Eleanor Roosevelt

Let's talk about fear.

We cannot ignore the fact that many women experience fear when it comes to investing. The question I hear time and time again, especially from first-time investors, is, "How do I overcome my fear?" If you think you're the only one who is scared to death when it comes time to buy that first rental property or to invest in that first business, or anytime you commit your hard-earned money to any investment, please know *you are not alone.*

The Upside and Downside of Fear

What's the best thing about fear?

Fear has its upside. Fear alerts us to possible life-threatening situations. You may feel fear when you hear a strange noise late at night. Thinking someone may have broken into your house, you immediately take any necessary precautions. Fear may set in when you find yourself walking alone through an unlit park at night, so you quickly find the safest route out. If you're driving in the middle of a snowstorm with almost zero

While fear can warn us of life-threatening events, it can also be a killer – a killer of dreams, of opportunities, of our own personal growth and passion, of living our life to its absolute fullest.

visibility fear may cause you to pull off the road until the storm subsides. So there is a markedly positive side to fear.

There is also a destructive side to fear. While fear can warn us of life-threatening events, it can also be a killer – a killer of dreams, of opportunities, of our own personal growth and passion, of living our life to its absolute fullest.

Whenever we enter into an arena that is unfamiliar and unknown, a little fear can be a good thing. A little fear can motivate us to take one extra in-depth look at the numbers on that rental property, or to tune in to the special TV report about the industry in which we just bought stocks. A touch of fear can keep us on our toes and sometimes avoid costly mistakes. This is where fear can serve us.

The harmful face of fear is when fear paralyzes us. When we're immobilized so we do nothing. We say "no" to the opportunity automatically, without even thinking. All we can see are all the things that will go wrong. We can spew out all the reasons why the investment is a bad, risky, and unwise venture to undertake. The fear of making mistakes, of losing money, and of personal disappointment wins.

So why do we allow fear to stop us? Two reasons why this happens are:

"I'm Going To Die!"

One of the functions of the mind, via fear, is to warn us of life-threatening situations. However, the mind often perceives something to be life-threatening, when it's not. For example, here is one mind talking:

> *"Investing is risky! I'm going to lose money! What if I can't pay my bills?! What if I can't pay my mortgage?! The bank will foreclose on my house! Then I'll be homeless! I'll be out on the streets. Oh my god, I'm going to die!"*

Whew! That's a lot of chatter. Yet, that's the kind of trick the mind can play. Are we really going to die if we make one investment? Of course not. But it's these automatic, unconscious responses that sometimes run our lives.

When you feel this paralyzing fear take over as you're looking at a new and unfamiliar investment opportunity, first acknowledge to yourself that this is not a life-threatening situation. This is not a do-or-die scenario. Second, rationally go through the pros and cons. What is the upside? What is the downside? How can you reduce the downside? In other words, move your irrational, reflexive mind out of the way.

Fear As An Excuse

A second and more evident reason that fear takes control is that when fear pops up it's simply easier not to face the fear. When we're facing something unknown, something that is going to challenge us or pressure us, it's uncomfortable. The easy thing to do is to do nothing.

For instance, have you ever had to give a talk in public? Experts say that people's number-one fear is the fear of public speaking. If you have that fear, then the easiest thing to do is to not go through that fear and to not give the talk.

The harder thing to do would be to confront your fear, to write your talk, to practice, to take a public speaking course, to practice some more, and then to finally step up on that stage. By going through that process you grow. By walking away from it you get smaller.

Can you think of one thing right now that you know that if you did it, even though it would be scary and uncomfortable, your life would be better and fuller because you went through it? (Maybe it's buying that first or next investment.) These are times when fear can either propel you forward or become an excuse to do nothing. At these moments you make a choice to either take it on and face your fear or to opt out, shy away, and stay where you are. In reality we never stay as we are, we either grow or we shrink. With the world moving and changing so fast, the choices we make either expand our lives or contract our lives. I don't believe there is an in-between.

Fear As An Asset

Fear can be the greatest asset we have. Every time fear comes up, and you're clear it's not life-threatening, that means you have an opportunity to grow and to expand yourself. It's often through this type of agitated process that we grow the most. And when you come through it it's exhilarating! You are not the same person you were before the process.

Think of it this way: *fear is how we grow.* Instead of dreading fear, look it straight in the eye and know you've just uncovered your next level of growth… if you so chose to seize it.

Ralph Waldo Emerson changed my life with this quote:

> *"He who is not every day conquering some fear has not learned the secret of life."*

Two Kinds Of Pain

The saddest words I hear from people as they get older is, "If only I had (fill in the blank)…" "I wish I had done (fill in the blank)…" They knew there was something more for them but, usually because of fear, they held back. The fear may be the fear of failure or the fear they might not find something better or the fear of losing or the fear of being humiliated. Whatever the fear, the fear was more powerful than the opportunity of a more passionate, joyful, self-fulfilling life. I heard Anthony Robbins, the motivational speaker, say from the stage, "There are two kinds of pain; the pain of failure and the pain of regret."

I'll choose the pain of failure every day. For me, the pain of regret is the worst punishment I can inflict upon myself. I know when I wimp out. I know when I quit. The bottom line is that in those moments that I held back I had a choice. And I chose to be a *coward*, instead of choosing *courage*.

No one has to tell me when I don't go for it. I'm well aware of those moments. And it's looking back on those times when the pain of regret is most piercing.

For some women the regret is giving up their careers. For others, it's allowing their careers to come between them and their families. And the classic regret is staying in an unfulfilling relationship or marriage because it is "easy" and "comfortable."

The one regret I hope *none* of us will ever face is the regret of ignoring our own financial interests and allowing someone else to dictate what they think is best for us.

No doubt it takes courage to make bold changes in your life. It takes courage to face the unknown. The good news is that whenever we choose courage over cowardice then we win – because we expand who we are. And then there can be no regrets.

A Moment Of Courage

I bet most of us can recall a courageous moment we each faced as a young girl or one we witnessed. I was watching a 7-year-old the other day and it brought back memories.

She was preparing to jump off the high diving board at the community swimming pool for the first time. I watched her as she climbed the ladder, clenching the railing tightly. She took that last step onto the diving board. She stared at the end of the board. Nothing else exists. She stood there, fixated, for what seemed an eternity. Then she took her first step forward, still holding firm to the railing. The railing ends, and now it's just her, the board, and the water below, which probably seemed like a mile away.

Very hesitantly she walked to the end of the board, her legs a little shaky. And then came the moment of truth – she was either going to take that huge, scary leap into the water far below or she was going to turn around, march back to the ladder, climb down, and say, "I can't do it."

She stands there for another couple of minutes and then with all the courage she can muster, she takes a deep breath, closes her eyes, and jumps off the board into the unknown.

There's a splash as she hits the water. When her head pops out of the water she has the biggest, brightest smile from ear to ear. "I did it!" She screams. She is ecstatic! She was scared to death, but she did it. And what does she want to do next? Climb back up that ladder and jump off that high-dive again… and again… and again.

That 7-year-old is really no different than you or me. The situation may be different, but the intensity of the fear and terror just before the decision to jump or not jump, whether into a pool or a new adventure, is very familiar.

"How Do I Overcome My Fear?"

When it comes to investing we're often stepping into unknown territory. For many of us, we are doing something we have never done before. We may not have the experience. We certainly do not have all the answers. I don't know any investor who does. So the learning curve is steep. The probability of making mistakes is high. And we're playing with real money, which always adds a bit of drama to the formula.

Our fear can come in many forms. It could be the fear of losing money. It might be the fear of making mistakes (which you really don't have to be fearful of because it's already a given – you will make mistakes.) Or maybe you've heard, as I have, that one of the greatest fears for women is the fear of ending up as a bag lady on the streets, broke and homeless. (And if you look at some of those previously mentioned statistics about elderly women and their money, that fear may be somewhat justified.) Whatever the fear, if it's there, admit it's there.

One way to *reduce* the fear, of course, is through education and experience. The more you learn and know about a certain investment, the more confident you are with your decisions. The more investments you own, the more self-assured and knowledgeable you become. Hence, fear will play a smaller role with every investment.

A Life-Changing Exercise

Most of us will experience fear, if not downright terror, at times. So how do we overcome it? I participated in an outdoors survival course years ago that was all about handling fear. On one of the exercises I had to climb to the top of a wooden pole, similar to a telephone pole, stand on top of the pole without using my hands and then leap out and grab onto a trapeze hanging free. I instantly thought the scariest part, by far, would be that leap of faith toward the trapeze. Not so. As I climbed up the pole grabbing and then stepping on each rung, I thought to myself, "This isn't so bad." Then I got to that last rung, which meant the only place for my hands to go was on the top flat surface of the pole that measured maybe 12 inches in diameter. Terror was about to strike. I now had two hands on the top of the pole, and my feet were on two rungs below. The scariest step of this entire exercise was, with no hands, taking my foot off of the rung and stepping on top of the pole. I was paralyzed. It seemed like an eternity that I was glued in that one position. Finally the instructor called up to me, "What's happening?"

I asked him, "How do I overcome my fear?"

He came back with, "This is not about getting rid of your fear. It's about learning how to *manage* your fear when it comes up. Just take the next step."

I have to tell you it took everything I had at that moment to bring my one foot on top of that pole and then move my other foot up next to it. I stood on that tiny platform, which barely fit my two feet, with my arms stretched out to my side for balance. "I did it." I thought. Then fear number-two set in. Now I had to leap straight out, and the goal was to grab onto a trapeze that was about six feet in front of me. I just repeated what my instructor told me, "This is about managing your fear. Just take the next step."

With that I took a long, deep breath, sprung off the pole, leaped into the air and caught the trapeze. As they lowered me to the ground my body was shaking more than when I started. My instructor walked over to me and asked, "Did you get the lesson?" Throughout every cell in my body, I got the lesson.

Facing The Fear Of My First Investment

Was I in total fear when I sat in the title company's office, papers in front of me, ready to sign for my first rental property? I was terrified.

In 1989 Robert, sounding like a survival class instructor himself, said to me, "Kim, it's time you start investing."

"Investing? What do you mean by investing?" I asked, totally confused.

Robert briefly explained some of his Rich Dad's principles to me about investing and real estate, and then he said, "Now it's up to you to figure it out."

"Oh, no!" I thought. "He wants me to climb to the top of that pole again!"

And thus my investing education began.

The one suggestion Robert made to me was, "Check out the neighborhood." So I did just that. A few blocks from where we lived in Eastmoreland, near Portland, Oregon, was a neighborhood called Westmoreland. It was a wonderful community filled with many small, cute homes with yards and porches. The area centered around a park, and the antique shops and restaurants had more of an old town feel to them.

To make a long story short, I came across this quaint two-bedroom, one-bath house that was for sale. It had a nice backyard and a separate garage. It even had a cute painted metal butterfly attached to the front of the house. Perfect. The purchase price was $45,000. I had to put down $5,000. And after doing all my calculations I figured I would make between $50 and $100 per month cash flow. Cash flow means that I collect the rent from the tenant, I pay the bills (such as taxes, insurance, water, etc.), I pay the mortgage payment, and the money remaining is my cash flow that goes directly to my pocket.

Since this was my very first real estate deal I really didn't know what I was doing. So I checked everything three or four times – the roof, the plumbing, the structure of the building, the taxes, the insurance – everything possible. I talked with several property managers to see what the property would rent for. I was thorough.

And still, when it came time to sign the closing papers at the title company's office and turn over my $5,000, my hand was shaking so much from fear that I could barely sign the papers. I did all my homework on this property. I checked it up one side and down the other. I triple-checked all my numbers. So why was I so scared? I kept saying to myself, "Just take the next step."

Again, this was my first investment real estate purchase. I just wasn't sure if my analysis of everything was correct. I did the best I could to figure it out. "But what if I made a mistake?" I thought. "What if I did something wrong in figuring out the numbers? What if, instead of making money every month, I lose money? What if there's a big plumbing or roofing problem? What if I lose my $5,000?" All these thoughts were running through my head as I sat at the closing table, staring at my $5,000 check I was about to hand over.

"Maybe I should just walk away from this deal." I said to myself. "That would be the easiest thing to do. Maybe I need to learn more about real estate before buying something. If this is such a good deal why isn't everyone clamoring to buy it?" Every one of those thoughts sounded like a reasonable excuse to back out of the deal. I could find plenty of people who would validate my decision to walk away.

But then I said to myself, "Kim, you've done as much research as you can do on this property. It seems to make sense from what you know. If you don't go through with this deal you will probably never invest in real estate. It's now or never. Take the leap and grab the bar." And with that, I signed the closing papers, turned over my check for the down payment, and I was the proud owner of my first investment property.

Did I make mistakes on this property? Yes. Did the mistakes cost me money? Yes. Did my numbers go exactly to plan? No. Was this my most important investment ever? Absolutely. It was my first. It got me off the starting blocks. It opened the first door that then led to more and more investments.

Was I scared and nervous at the next closing and the next closing and the next? Yes, I was. In fact there was one real estate closing where I was literally crying with fear because I was sure the property was about to fall down. I got through that one too. And with each new investment I learned a little more and a little more. I got a little smarter. Gained more knowledge. It truly is a process that you take one step at a time.

In Chapter 20 I'll explain the one investment deal that forever eliminated 95 percent of my fear, and why it did so. It is one of my great life lessons.

An Investor's Story – "Taking That Next Step"

The following is an inspiring story from a woman who faced her fears on her first investment property. As a result she is a happy and successful investor today.

Vida's Story:

My husband and I were true small business owners. We were running very fast but getting nowhere. In fact we were falling further behind each month.

I was 47 years old with two kids in college and three at home. It was difficult finding the time I needed to study, seek out knowledge, and look for potential real estate deals. But somehow I made the time because I knew how important this would be for me and my family. My husband was very supportive, and we enjoyed learning together. We decided that I would focus on real estate while he would study other investments such as stocks and options.

It was a huge responsibility for me when the time came to close on our first investment property, an apartment building. It would take our entire savings to complete the deal, and I was scared to death. By the hour I would change my mind about going through with it. There is no doubt that I would have talked myself out of it if it were not for the support of some key people around me.

I had to keep telling myself that I had invested a lot of money and time in my financial education in the past two years and that I did know what I was doing. I repeated this to myself over and over to drown out that little voice that was constantly screaming at me saying that I did not know what the hell I was doing and how could I ever think this would work, and that I was going to lose all my family's money, etc. etc. etc.

Today I can look back and laugh, and that is a great feeling. I went through with the deal, and that property is completely full with tenants and is generating a very nice cash flow. I have and will continue to learn and to buy more investment properties. I just get smarter and more confident, and I have more fun.

Chapter Eleven

HOW WEALTHY ARE YOU?

"Women will always be dependent until she holds a purse of her own."
– Elizabeth Cady Stanton
women's rights activist (1815-1902)

One morning I opened my e-mail, and I recognized an address I hadn't seen in a while. The e-mail message read:

"Hi, Kim! It's me, Janice! I'm going to be in Phoenix tomorrow for a spur-of-the-moment one-day trip. Are you available for a quick lunch? Ciao! Janice"

I responded:

"Hi, Janice! Tomorrow would be perfect. I'd love to catch up with you and hear what you've been up to. Cheers, Kim"

We decided on a time and place.

In her last e-mail to me Janice wrote excitedly:

"Kim, I've been thinking a lot about what we talked about in New York. I'm beginning to understand it more and more, especially as I work day-in and day-out in my business. I'm anxious to talk more about it. See you tomorrow! Ciao, Janice"

The next day I knew she must have been excited to talk because for the first time that I can remember Janice was seated at the table as I walked in. She actually arrived early! She was saying good-bye to someone on her cell phone as I approached the table.

She jumped up and we gave each other a big hug. "You look mah-ve-lous," she laughed.

"I'm so glad you called," I said. "You, of course, look fabulous as always."

From then on the lunch was like a blur. We talked nonstop for almost two hours. I know we ate something, but food was not the focus of our get-together.

I started, "So tell me what's been happening."

"Money Runs Me!"

"My mind has been spinning since we last saw each other. I undoubtedly do not have it all worked out, but I'm beginning to see glimpses of what my life might look like if money were not an issue. I never realized how many of my decisions are based on simply making more money versus what is best for me and my business," Janice confessed.

"For example," she went on, "last week I had a choice to make. There were two events I could attend but both were on the same day so I had to choose between the two. One event was more of a networking and educational day with some of the top people in the retail industry. This was the program I truly wanted to attend. The other event was like a mini trade show where I could actually sell my products."

"Tell me what you did," I said curiously.

"My entire decision process had nothing to do with what would be best for the long-term of my business," she said, frustrated. "The whole decision came down to what will make me more money today. So I chose the trade show."

"And?" I prompted.

Janice continued. "The trade show was basically a waste of time. I sold very little. The people attending were not really my customers. And I didn't enjoy it. Instead I could have attended the full-day program where I later learned I could have met and asked questions of two of my top business "heroes," who were not advertised to be there. The feedback from my friends who attended was phenomenal. I felt I could have learned so many things that would have been great for the future growth of my company. But me, I went for the quick, short-term bucks."

"Pretty good lesson," I commented.

"Again, it was a small glimpse of what my life could be like if the choices I make were not so dependent on how much money I'll make today," she said. "What I'm starting to grasp hold of is if I knew my basic living expenses were covered and not dependent on my business then my business would be so much more fun because I would make the decisions that were in the long-term best interest of my business… and my life."

"Yesterday I turned down breakfast with a woman who is doing what I want to be doing in about two years. What did I do instead? I had a meeting with my three key sales people because our sales were down last month," she said. "Now I know those sales meetings are important. The stupid thing is I could have had that meeting later that day or even the next morning. But I may never have the opportunity again to meet face-to-face with this woman who could truly propel my business. And that is just stupid."

"So, what's your plan from here?" I asked.

"Well I feel that I now have a genuine reason why I want to get started and work toward what you call financial independence. I want my business to be fun. I want it to be a place where I learn and grow and those with whom I work learn and develop and pursue their dreams and goals as I am pursuing mine. That, to me, would be so exciting and fulfilling." I could see the passion in her eyes as she spoke.

"That is a compelling reason why," I acknowledged.

Janice and I kept talking.

I shared with her my conversation with Leslie about how she thought she wasn't smart enough, primarily because of the language used by "the experts." We discussed the importance of learning the vocabulary, or the jargon, of money, investing, and finance.

"That is key," Janice agreed. "Because when I hear all that mumbo jumbo I just check out. And then I lose interest in the subject altogether."

We spent a good part of our lunch discussing what financial

independence is and why the primary focus is on cash flow.

The Next Step

"So where do I go from here? What's my next step?" Janice pressed.

"Remember earlier I said that the number-one goal of financial independence is to get more cash flow coming in, without working, than is going out, in the way of living expenses?" I asked.

"Yes, I love that idea," she answered. "And what else I love is that you said you don't need a huge amount of money to be financially free, which I always thought was the only way to accomplish it."

"That's right. Financial independence, according to the formula I use, thanks to Robert's Rich Dad, is different for everyone. The amount of cash flow you need to be financially free will be different than the amount your neighbor or best friend would need."

I shared with Janice how Robert and I became financially free in 1994. "It took us only five years to become financially free. Remember, I told you about my very first investment property I bought in 1989: a little two-bedroom, one-bath house? Well, five years later, as a result of our cash flow investments, which were primarily in real estate, we had a total of $10,000 per month flowing into our pockets. That's not a lot of money but the beauty of it was that our living expenses at the time were only $3,000. So at that point we were free. We no longer had to work for the money to cover that $3,000 per month. Instead, money was now working for us, and $10,000 cash was flowing into our pockets each month."

"Think about it," I began. "To be financially free and independent would mean that you never again have to work for money because every month you have enough money coming in from your investments to cover your living expenses. So your wealth is infinite because it never runs out."

Janice jumped in, "So my next step is then to figure out how much cash flow I need to cover my living expenses. I need to calculate what my monthly expenses are."

"That's it! We can do that right now if you want."

"Let's do it," she said and pounded her fist on the table.

Determining Your Wealth

"OK, let's find out how wealthy you are," I said.

"What exactly is your definition of wealth?" Janice asked.

"Great question," I replied. "The word wealth has countless definitions. I use the definition that was introduced to me years ago. The definition comes from a brilliant inventor, philosopher, and humanitarian, named R. Buckminster Fuller. Fuller's definition of wealth is:

'A person's ability to survive X number of days forward.'

"Put into financial terms the question is, how many days could you survive without working? And the key words are *without working*. If you stopped working today, which means your income from work stops as well, how long could you survive on the amount of money you have?"

"How exactly do you figure that out?" Janice asked.

"It's actually pretty simple," I answered. "First you add up all of your living expenses. This is what it costs you to 'survive' each month. If you had no salary or income from your business, how much money would you need each month to live on?"

"Do you mean what are my bare-bone expenses I could live on? Because I could eliminate eating out, which I do regularly, or get by with a lot less shopping," Janice explained.

I'm so glad you brought that up because this is an important distinction. This formula is based upon your current standard of living. I am not talking about moving into a smaller house or trading in your car and riding the bus. I am not a proponent of 'living below your means.' Why would you want to be financially independent if you had to cut back to a lifestyle you don't enjoy? Financial freedom is about living at the standard of living you want. So today you have a current standard of living, and those are the expenses we are going to use. You can always increase your standard of living in the future… which I highly recommend."

STEP #1 – How Wealthy Are You?

Janice nodded happily. "So if I'm to add up my expenses they would include the following items."

Janice made up her list on the spot. This is what it looked like.

Mortgage Payment	$2,500
Property Taxes	300
Home Insurance	150
General House Expenses (utilities, water, phone, cable)	350
Car Payment	550
Gas	150
Meals & Entertainment (dine in and out)	500
Misc. Purchases (clothes, home items)	500
Magazine/Newspapers/Books	50
Travel/Vacations	250

As you put together your own list of living expenses, here is a list of possible expenses you might include.

- Mortgage Payment
- Property Taxes
- Home Insurance
- General House Expenses – utilities, water, phone, cable
- Rent
- Car Payment(s)
- Car maintenance
- Gas
- Transportation Expense (train, bus, taxi)

- Meals – in-house
- Meals – dine-out
- Entertainment – shows, concerts, sports events, etc.
- Miscellaneous Purchases –
    clothes, household items, books, hair care, etc.
- Magazine/Newspaper Subscriptions
- Travel/Vacations
- Children:
    Babysitter
    Schooling
    Clothing
    Miscellaneous purchases
    Sports/Lessons
- Medical Insurance
- Exercise/Gym Expense
- Pet Expenses (food, medical, boarding)
- Yard Maintenance
- Other Vehicle Expenses (boat, motorcycle, RV)
- Educational Programs
- Parking Expense
- Any other expenses you incur

After looking over Janice's list I asked, "So what's your total amount of monthly expenses?"

"$4,900 per month," she announced.

"And were you pretty honest in your numbers?" I probed.

"Well," she hesitated, "I probably spend a little more on clothes and on entertainment. I should probably bump those figures up a bit. It might be good to put in a category for 'reserves' or 'miscellaneous' since unexpected things do come up."

"Great idea," I lauded. "The more honest you can be with yourself around your numbers the greater your chance of success in achieving your goal."

I added, "When Robert and I were broke, the hardest thing for me to do was meet with my bookkeeper twice a month. It was not a pleasant experience to sit down with her at each meeting and face the truth of how little money we had coming in and how much we had going out, as well as all the outstanding debts. But I have to admit by being honest about where we were, that allowed us to set clear goals and deal with each creditor and situation that came up. Had we lied to ourselves about where we were financially we might still be handling those debts."

"I got it," Janice responded.

She made a few adjustments to her number and then announced, "My monthly expenses are $5,300."

"Well done," I congratulated her. "That is step number one to finding out how wealthy you are. Ready for step two?" I asked.

"Absolutely," Janice replied.

STEP #2 – How Wealthy Are You?

"The next step is to calculate how much money you currently have, *not including your salary from your job or work.* In other words, if you stopped working today how much money do you have in savings, CDs, stocks that could be sold or liquidated immediately – and, of course, cash flow generated from assets."

"What about my jewelry or my grandmother's silver pieces? Don't those count?" Janice asked.

"I don't count those types of items for two reasons," I explained. "First, I don't know if I can sell them. If I can they are probably worth much less than I would anticipate. And second, the exercise is to assume your current standard of living. If you begin selling everything you can then you lower your standard of living."

"That makes sense," Janice admitted. "OK, let me put my list together, which won't take long at all."

When all was said and done, Janice came up with the following list:

Savings	$18,000
Stocks	6,000

"That's my list." Janice declared. "I knew it would be quick. The bottom line is that I have a total of $24,000 that would be available."

STEP #3 – How Wealthy Are You?

"Good," I said. "Now simply divide the $24,000 that you have into your monthly expenses of $5,300 and what do you come up with?"

Janice reached into her briefcase and pulled out a calculator. "That's $24,000 divided by $5,300. That equals 4.5," Janice said, looking a little puzzled. "What does that mean?"

"That means that you are four-and-a-half months wealthy. If you stopped working today you have enough money to cover your living expenses for four and a half months."

I watched as Janice's shoulders slumped. She looked at me somewhat stunned and said, "That's not very long. I never looked at it that way before."

"There is no right or wrong answer here," I pointed out. "This is simply your starting point. For many people today, if they stopped working they have zero wealth, or worse, negative wealth."

"So the equation is I take the money I have saved up and divide that number into what my monthly living expenses are. Is that correct?" She asked.

"It's that simple. And we'll get into the missing piece of the puzzle in a minute," I said. "But let's say a person's monthly expenses are $2,500 per month. She has $5,000 in savings. That $5,000 divided by $2,500 equals 2, which means she can pay for her current lifestyle for two months.

"Now for the missing piece," I continued. "The full equation is this." I wrote it on a napkin.

Savings (or available cash)

+ income coming in without you working /
   monthly living expenses

= Your Wealth

"And I obviously don't have any money coming in that I don't have to work for. That's the missing piece, isn't it?" Janice concluded. "So what is the goal? Is your wealth number supposed to be for as many months as you think you will live? That would be a huge number!"

"What's The Goal?"

"That would be a huge number," I agreed. "But you ask an excellent question. To be financially independent your wealth would be infinite."

"Infinite?" she asked confused.

"Think about it, "I began. "To be financially free and independent would mean that you never again have to work for money because every month you have enough money coming in from your investments to cover your living expenses. So your wealth is infinite because it never runs out."

"If I thought I needed $1,000,000 to live on for the rest of my life, then I would need to work really hard to save up that much money. That would take me a very long time to do, and I may never get there. And even if I did, that $1,000,000 will eventually get used up, and then I'm in big trouble."

"That's exactly what I'm talking about," I said.

"So it's my expenses that determine the amount of *cash flow I* need. And now that I know what my expenses are I can set my goal for what my monthly amount of money coming in from my investments needs to be," she realized out loud.

"You got it!" I grinned. "It's called cash flow. Your cash is flowing in. And cash flow coming in from your investments is called *passive income*. It's passive because you're not working for it."

Janice said excitedly, "And my cash flow goal is that I want a cash flow of $5,300 per month coming in every month without working for it!"

"Yes, $5,300 per month... or more," I said.

"Or more," she agreed.

"Now the next question is how do you do that?"

"That's exactly what I was just about to ask!" she laughed. "But you actually explained it to me when you were talking about your investing formula. You said that you buy or create assets. Assets are investments that put money in my pocket. So my next step is to start learning about and finding assets that flow money to my pocket!" she said triumphantly.

Then Janice said, "I just have one last question before we go, I don't have much extra money lying around. You see how much I have in savings. Don't you have to have money in order to make money? Doesn't it take a lot of money to get into the game of investing?"

"Terrific question," I replied. "I know we both have to run, so let's take up this subject later this week by phone."

As we were walking out of the restaurant I said to Janice, "Let me just say this on your question about money. Not having the money can be one of your greatest benefits when it comes to investing. We'll talk soon! Ciao!"

Chapter Twelve

"I Don't Have the Money!"

"Money can't buy happiness, but it can make you awfully comfortable while you're being miserable."
    – *Clare Boothe Luce*

I was planning a trip to New York City, and I remembered telling Leslie that I'd contact her on my next visit. I dialed her cell phone number.

"Hello?" Leslie answered.

"Hi, Leslie! This is Kim. Do you have a couple of minutes to talk?"

"Of course!" she replied.

"Hey, I'm going to be in New York in about two weeks. Do you want to get together?" I asked.

"As long as we can do lunch!" she laughed.

I smiled. "I guess lunch is our thing. Janice was in town a few days ago, so we got together… for lunch, of course."

We talked for several minutes and decided on a day and time. "You pick the place," I suggested.

"I've got a favorite place. I'll check if it's available and let you know" she responded. We hung up.

Another Lunch With The Girls

Leave it to the artist to come up with such a unique spot for lunch, I thought as I walked to where we were meeting.

I pulled out my cell phone, since I wasn't sure exactly where this 'favorite spot' of Leslie's was. "Hi, Leslie! I'm crossing the bridge. Do I go right or left?" I asked.

"Go right, follow the path, and you'll see us. You can't miss it. Gorgeous day isn't it?" she said.

I laughed to myself as I walked. There wasn't a cloud in the sky. It was warm enough that I only needed a light jacket. As I came around the bend, sure enough, there she was. Sitting in the middle of a big bright red blanket laid out on the grass in the middle of Central Park, with a large picnic basket next to her, grinning from ear to ear.

I waved as I walked quickly toward her. I was surprised to see another woman sitting next to her with her back to me. She didn't move when Leslie waved back to me.

As I came up close to them I recognized the other woman immediately. "Tracey! What is the world are you doing here?" I exclaimed. We gave each other a big hug.

"I was so disappointed to miss the last reunion you all had that when you said you were coming to town, Leslie called me and asked if I could join you," she said. "I wasn't about to miss another opportunity to reconnect, especially after Leslie told me how much fun you all had together."

We spent the next hour catching up with one another… and eating a fabulous picnic lunch that Leslie put together. Tracey told us how burned out she is with her job in Chicago. "My life is not a life," she said with an air of regret. "I'm working more than ever, but I'm not seeing the rewards of all the hard work. I get pay raises, but I don't seem to get ahead. My husband works as much as I do. We have two kids – one in high school, one in seventh grade. I do my best to juggle everything, but, to be honest, at the end of the day I just don't feel that we're making progress. I'm running at full speed just in order to keep up. I'm really ready for a change.

"What really frightened me," she added, "is that a couple of months ago my husband's company was sold, and there was a possibility that he was going to be fired because the company that bought his company was replacing many of the employees with their own employees. Thank goodness he wasn't fired, because that would have been a huge blow to our income. But it showed me just how vulnerable we are regarding our finances."

Leslie jumped in, "I shared some of the conversations we've been having about money and becoming financially free, and it seemed to strike a chord with Tracey."

"As you can tell, the timing couldn't be better for me," Tracey admitted.

As with all of our girl lunches we yakked incessantly. Tracey spoke about how difficult it's been to manage a career and a family. I joked with her and recited a quote I heard from Gloria Steinem, the feminist activist and founder of *Ms. Magazine:* "I have yet to hear a man ask for advice on how to combine marriage and a career."

We all laughed… and then went a bit quiet as we realized just how true that statement is.

Tracey said, "I think that's why the thought that 'I don't have the time' seems to dictate so much of my life. Whenever anyone suggests *anything* that is going to take even a minute of my precious time those words automatically fly out of my mouth. I noticed that was the first thing that went through my mind when Leslie talked about your conversation about money and investing. But I feel so out of control that I need to make a drastic change. That's one of the reasons why I'm here today."

Déjà Vu… A Familiar Question

Tracey's reason *why* was already starting to unfold. We covered a lot of ground in a short period of time. Then Tracey raised a very familiar question. She asked, "But don't you need money in order to invest – don't you first need money in order to make money?"

I grinned. "We should get Janice on the phone because that's the exact question she asked as we were leaving the restaurant the other day. We didn't have time to get into it."

Tracey spoke up. "I'm really embarrassed to admit this, but after all these years of busting our you-know-what's, my husband and I have so little put aside. We have our 401(k)s and a couple of mutual funds, plus a small account set aside for our kids' education, but other than that we spend just about everything, sometimes more, that we make."

"If it makes you feel better, Tracey, you're in much better shape than me," Leslie confessed.

"So doesn't it take money to make money?" Tracey asked again.

"Let me just say this, and this is what I left Janice with after our lunch," I began. "Not having the money was the best thing for me when I started investing."

The two women looked at me, puzzled.

"How could that be?" Leslie asked. "I'm with Tracey, I think I have to have money in order to invest."

"But do you need the money before you start *looking?*" I countered.

"I don't get your point," Tracey said.

I replied, "Have you ever said the words, 'As soon as I have the money then I will do such-and-such,' or 'When I have some free time then I'll do X'? Do either of those lines sound familiar?"

Tracey answered. "Yes. I've certainly said those things, especially the line about free time. So what?"

"Do you ever find the free time?" I probed.

She thought about it for a few seconds and then admitted, "Almost never."

Leslie cut in. "I say, 'As soon as I have some money' quite a bit. And you know what? Those things I'm going to do once I have the money never seem to happen. And you know why? Because the money always seems to go to something else. It's almost like saying those words guarantees that it's not going to happen."

"That's the point," I said. "When I hear someone say, 'I'll start as soon as I have the money,' then I'm just about certain they will never start. That thought alone, 'as soon as I have the money,' justifies you not doing anything because you can't… until you have the money. It's a great excuse to do nothing."

"So if I have little-to-no money to begin investing, what do I do?" Tracey asked somewhat frustrated.

"Can I tell you a story that, for me, changed my thinking that I first need the money in order to invest?" I asked.

Tracey and Leslie nodded.

"We Have No Money"

"When Robert and I lived in Oregon and I was just starting my investing career we had no money saved up. In fact we had very little money period. Paying our bills each month was an adventure in itself. One afternoon we returned from a five-week business trip in Australia. We had literally just walked through the front door, suitcases still in hand, when the phone rang. It was our real estate broker. He said we had one hour to look at this 12-unit apartment building that he had listed that very moment. We were the first people he called. If he didn't hear from us in one hour then he would offer it to the next investor on his list. Coming off of 24 hours of traveling, we were exhausted. Robert said, 'I'll go check it out.' I still remember the words I yelled as he got into the car, knowing our dismal financial status, 'Don't buy it!'

"So, of course, Robert came back all excited, and the first words out of his smiling mouth were, 'I bought it!'

"My mouth dropped to the floor. 'What? We don't have the money!' I said automatically.

"'Well, if we don't come up with the money then we won't buy it,' he said. 'But let's figure out how we could come up with the money. I signed the offer, which the seller accepted, that says we have two weeks to do our inspection of the property, including the financials. If we don't like what we see then we are free to walk away from the deal. But that also means we have two weeks to figure out how to come up with the money.'

"I have to admit I was more than a little apprehensive.

"We got the financial information on the property from the broker. We then called our friend Drew in Canada who was a very successful real estate investor. He said he was interested so I faxed him the numbers. We needed $50,000 for the down payment on this property that was selling for $330,000. Within one hour of faxing Drew the numbers he called and said, 'I really like this property. This is a great deal. I'm in for 50 percent.' This meant that he would put up $25,000 and he would own half of the apartment building along with us. Now we just needed to come up with the other $25,000.

"'Great!' Robert said. 'I'll call you tomorrow with more information.'

"We were driving when we got Drew's call. It was at the moment Drew said, "I'm in" something peculiar and at the same time exhilarating came over me. I turned to Robert and said, 'If Drew, whose life is real estate investing, thinks this is such a hot deal, then it must be good.'

"Robert agreed.

"I grinned and said, 'Let's do the deal ourselves. Let's own 100 percent!'

"Robert hit the brakes and pulled the car to the side of the road. 'Look,' he said impatiently, 'Drew is willing to put up half the money that leaves only $25,000 to go. If we buy this property ourselves, then we're back at square one.' There was silence. But both our minds were chattering away. We both looked at each other, and then Robert said, 'OK. Let's go for it.'

"Now, many people might think what we did was a pretty stupid thing to do. We thought that at times ourselves. We were turning down a sure thing and could have ended end up with nothing. It was all or nothing.

"We were back at the beginning, looking for $50,000. We went from bank to bank, and they all turned us down. We approached people we knew and asked if they would lend us the money at a reasonable rate of interest – no luck. We then went through our own finances with a fine-tooth comb and came up with a small amount of the money needed. We turned to our business and came up with some new ideas that would generate additional sales immediately before we were to close on this property. All in all we were able to pull together a total of $25,000. I thought to myself, 'This is right where we were when Drew first said yes.'

"We kept going. We had three days left until our offer expired. As a last ditch effort we approached our own bank. We purposely avoided them in our first go-around with the banks because we only had about $3,500 total in our personal and business accounts so we assumed this bank would not be too receptive.

"Robert and I walked in and asked to speak to James, the bank manager. We had met James on several occasions. It was a small bank and he, like us, was new in town. We sat down at his desk. We explained the real estate deal to him. We showed him the financials and explained how we would pay back the loan from the cash flow from the property. James quietly turned to us and said, 'You two have a lot of guts coming in here. First of all, I know how much money you both have with our bank. Secondly, you've only been customers of our bank for two months.' We knew the bad news was coming.

"James went on, 'Even if I were, for just a brief moment, to consider this loan, which is very iffy, then the first step is I would need you both to sign this document. So why don't you at least do that?' he suggested.

"We figured he was doing his best to be polite and lessen the pain of the rejection that was sure to follow.

"We signed the document and handed it back to him. He took it and placed it in a manila file folder. Then he looked up at us with this grin on his face and said, 'Congratulations you just got your loan.'

"We were stunned. 'Really? You're giving us the loan?' I asked.

'The property makes sense,' he said. 'Plus I've only met you two a few times, but I can see how committed you are to your business, and I trust you are going to be as committed to your investments. Good luck.'

"And with that we walked out of the bank, still in amazement, called our broker, and went through with the deal… all 100 percent of it.

"Now, that bank manager had no logical reason for giving us that loan. How could we have ever guessed that he would have taken a chance on us? Sometimes the money pops up in the least expected places. Magic does happen. But the point is that we would have never found the money or bought the property had we not been driven by the actual apartment building and given a real deadline," I ended.

No Money? No Problem

"It sounds like what you're saying is the exact opposite of what I thought I should do," Leslie said. "Instead of finding the money first, you're saying find the investment first. Is that right?"

"That's just what I'm saying," I acknowledged. "Most people say, 'First I'll get the money, then I'll buy the investment.' Instead I've learned to say, 'First I'll find the investment, then I'll get the money.'"

"Keep going," Leslie said hesitantly.

"It's simple," I continued. "Find the investment first. Make it real to you. Get excited about it. For example, if it's a three-bedroom, two-bath rental property, look at it. Touch it. Walk through it. Figure out the cash flow. Envision owning it. Talk about it. Now it's no longer just an idea or a theory, it's for real. At that point your mind kicks into gear, and you'll be amazed at how creative you become in finding the financing. It's the same for an investment in a business or any other investment that excites you. Usually what excites me most, though, is the cash flow I see the investment paying me."

"So I find the investment first instead of finding the money first," Leslie repeated. "That means I can start right away. To be honest, I was getting a bit discouraged figuring out how I was going to come up with the money. All I could envision was me working harder. I got tired just thinking about it, which is why I never made any valiant effort to look for investments."

Tracey stepped in, "So are you saying that if I find a good investment the money will miraculously appear?"

"It won't appear if you just sit back, wait, and do nothing," I said. "You have to take action. You've got to go and find it. There are two things that work in your favor if you have a specific investment in your grasp. First, you are now motivated by an actual investment that you can talk about and present to lenders and potential investors. Second, you will usually have some sort of time limit for raising some or all of the money. There is now an urgency, a deadline, so you can't say, 'I'll work on that later.' It forces you to act immediately. The more people, potential lenders, and potential investors you talk to, the more energy you create, and the more energy you create, the more opportunities will open up to you. Energy attracts energy. That's when the magic happens... like that bank manager giving us a loan."

Leslie asked, "Do you find the money every time? Have you ever not found the money?"

"There definitely are no guarantees, but this way at least you're in the game. You've got a shot at it. Or you can say to yourself, 'I don't have the money. I can't afford it' and take yourself out of the game before it even starts. By going after the money the odds of you getting the investment might be 50 percent to 100 percent. But if you've already decided you can't afford it then your odds are zero."

Not Having Money Is A Benefit

Tracey questioned, "I understand about tracking the investment first. I'm not sure I understand how not having the money is a benefit. It seems like you went through a lot of effort to find the money."

"Good point," I replied. "It did take a lot of effort – as did the next deal and the deal after that. In fact, almost every investment we have made, we did not have the money we needed readily available. When I started investing, it was because we simply did not have much money. Today I don't have money because all of our money is always invested."

"And not having the money is a benefit because... " Tracey pushed.

"Because it forces you to think. It forces you to be creative. Instead of just having one strategy for financing my investments, such as using my own money, I now have countless ways to finance my investments. The most important benefit is that I will never let the excuse that I don't have money stop me from going after a good investment. It's amazing what you can do when you have to," I said.

"One of the greatest lessons Robert's Rich Dad taught him was to never say the words, 'I can't afford it.' Whenever you say the words 'I can't' your mind automatically shuts down. Instead of saying he couldn't afford something his Rich Dad would ask himself, 'How can I afford it?' By asking yourself that question your mind opens and searches for answers."

How To Find The Money

Most people's first stop for a loan or additional funds is at a traditional bank. When that first bank turns them down, they quit and say, "I can't get a loan." There's that word "can't" again. What they don't realize is that the bank they first approached does not loan money for the type of property or business they're pursuing. Different banks lend money for different types of investments. Aside from your traditional banks, here are just a few alternative methods for financing your investments. You'll discover additional ways to raise money as your investing experience grows.

– **Seller financing:** As with a rental property, the seller acts as the bank. You have a loan agreement with the seller that specifies the amount of the loan, the interest rate you will pay the seller, and the length or term of the loan.

– **Finance out of cash flow:** For example, you buy a business and you have an agreement with the seller, lender, or investor to pay them back through the cash flow that the business generates.

– **Lender financing:** There are many different types of lenders available. This is where a mortgage or business broker can be a valuable member of your team. These brokers know what lenders lend for which investments. The lender pays the fees of the broker. You do not.

– **Assumable loans:** In real estate, a property may have a loan attached to the property, which means you can simply "assume" the existing loan with little qualifying effort on your part. You must also assume the existing terms of the loan, which includes the interest rate, the term of the loan, and any other specifics.

– **Other investors:** They are many people with money but no interest, time, or expertise in finding and managing certain investments. If you can prove that your investment – be it real estate, a business, tax lien certificates, precious metals, whatever the investment, – will give the investor a good return on his or her money then individual investors may be a good source of financing for you.

– **Family and Friends:** You can approach your family or friends to invest with you. You put up the time and effort, and they put up the money. If you do approach your family or friends for financing, then here are two words of caution. 1) Treat your family and friends as investors, not as people who love and who will "help you out." If you're going to be an investor, then handle each investment professionally. Prove to your investors how they will get their money back and a good return on their money. Draw up agreements between you and them. 2) Because of the emotional relationship between you and your family and friends I don't necessarily recommend going this route. A strong friendship is not worth risking over an investment that may not perform. I've seen family fights where the brother-in-law who loaned his sister-in-law money desperately needed that money back seven months later and then the sister-in-law was scrambling to find new financing. It's not worth it. Treat every investment as a separate business because that is exactly what it is.

"There's Always Money"

I told my friends, "Just last week a broker with whom I work came to me with a real estate investment. After a few rounds my offer was accepted. This broker saw me scramble to come up with the down payment, which came from three different sources. I could tell he was a little nervous that I might not come through. The day we closed on that property I turned to him and said, 'Thanks for a great deal. Call me as soon as you come across another. Tomorrow would not be too early.'

"He looked at me and said, 'Tomorrow? But aren't you out of money? I thought this last deal used up all your funds?'

"I smiled confidently, 'I can always find the money for a great deal.'"

Tracey said, "So the bottom line is, I shouldn't focus on getting the money first. If I do, chances are I'll never get started. Instead I should concentrate on finding the investment first. Once I find the investment then I focus on finding the money. I like it."

"That's it," I replied. "Now let me share with you both one final tip that Robert and I have used for many, many years. This is how you can accumulate money every single day without making any drastic changes to what you're doing now. But first, pass the cheese plate."

Chapter Thirteen

MORE ABOUT THE MONEY

"A good goal is like a strenuous exercise – it makes you stretch."
– Mary Kay Ash

"So what's the hot tip?" Tracey asked.

"I'll tell you another story," I started. "Remember I told you about when Robert and I moved to Oregon, we had no savings and barely enough money to pay our bills?"

The two women nodded.

"It was at that time that we realized we needed to do something different or, financially, we'd always be behind the eight ball. Even though we were making very little money at that time we decided in order to have any kind of financial future we had to take steps toward that future today."

"So what did you do?" Leslie asked.

"The first thing we did was hire a bookkeeper," I told her.

"Why a bookkeeper?" she prodded. "You said you had hardly any money. Why would you need a bookkeeper if you had only a little money?"

"Do you know how easy it is to lie to yourself about your money?" I asked. "I used to think at that time that somehow our money problems would just miraculously work themselves out. Being the optimist that I am, the last thing I wanted to do was to face our financial dilemma. 'If I don't think about it, it will just go away' was my mantra."

Leslie laughed, "Are you a mind reader? That's exactly what I do."

"It's a lot easier than facing the truth, isn't it?" I replied. "So the hardest thing I could do was to hire a bookkeeper who met with me twice a month. Every two weeks Betty would shove our gloomy financial facts in my face. It was like a mother who won't let her child leave the table until she's eaten her green beans. Betty would not let me leave our meeting until every bill and every dollar (or lack of dollar) was addressed and accounted for. It was not pleasant. I dreaded each meeting."

"Is there an upside to this story?" Tracey poked fun at me.

I laughed. "The upside was that I knew where we stood financially. I wasn't pretending everything was fine or that things would simply work out. I knew the truth about our income and our expenses. And once we knew where we were, then we could realistically begin to figure out where we wanted to go and how we were going to get there."

I continued. "Before Betty the bookkeeper I was like an ostrich hiding its head in the sand. It was no different then calling a restaurant and asking, 'How do I get to your restaurant?' but not telling them where you're coming from. If the restaurant hostess doesn't know where you are, then how can she direct you to where you want to go?

"So if you want to figure out where you want to go financially you've got to figure out where exactly you are today."

Hot Tip:

"In meeting with Betty every other week, the first thing Robert and I realized was that we were not putting anything aside for our future. Every penny we made was going to pay our bills... as best we could. So we committed to beginning to pay ourselves first and *then pay* our creditors. I realize the term 'pay yourself first' is almost cliché and means different things to different people. Here is what it means to us."

"Our plan was simple.

"For every dollar that came into our household, no matter where it came from, we first took 30 percent off the top. So if

$100 came in we took $30 off the top. If it was $1, then we took 30 cents.

"We then divided up the money into three accounts:

1. Investing Account (10 percent)

2. Savings Account (10 percent)

3. Charity or Tithing Account (10 percent)

"*After* we took the 30 percent off *then* the remaining monies went to pay bills. Paying ourselves first meant that that 30 percent went to building our financial future.

"The one key to this whole program is that you've got to stick with it. You can't say 'I'll skip it this month, but I'll do twice as much next month.' Chances are you won't catch up next month. The most important part of this process is the *discipline* or commitment to adhere to it for every dollar that comes in. It's not so much the percentage amount you put away every month, it's the *habit* of doing it again and again and again with every cent you receive. Once you've established the habit it becomes automatic.

"You may choose to use different percentages than we used. We chose 30 percent because we knew that was a bit of a stretch for us given our financial situation at the time. If you choose to go with a smaller percentage or amount that is fine. I do strongly caution you not to make it too easy on yourself for two reasons.

"First, if you make the percentages too light, then it will take you longer to see substantial results. Second, if you don't see good results quickly, then you may very well lose interest and discontinue the habit. I believe there has to be a bit of a stretch, a bit of a sacrifice, to make it worthwhile. Be creative. If you do this you'll be amazed at how quickly those accounts add up.

"The big thing we realized was that the 30 percent was our future. If we didn't start preparing for our financial future now then we'd have no future."

Tracey asked, "But if you were struggling to get by, how did you pay your bills?"

I started laughing. "That's exactly what our bookkeeper, Betty, asked! Our conversation went like this:

"I said, 'Betty, what we want to do is take 30 percent off the top for any and all money that comes in. That money goes into three bank accounts that we can only touch for investments and charities. The savings account is only for dire emergencies.'

"Betty said, 'You can't do that! You have bills to pay. How are you going to pay your bills?'

"I said, "We'll pay something to every creditor every month. Sometimes we may pay less than they ask for. If I have to I'll get on the phone to them and explain that we guarantee we will pay them 100 percent but we may have to stretch it out just a bit longer."

"Betty said, "I have a better idea. Why don't we pay your bills fully, and then we'll set aside anything that's left over."

"I said, "That's what everyone says they'll do. The problem is there is never anything left over. Let's stick with this plan, and I'll handle the creditors."

"Betty groaned.

"So weren't your creditors hounding you day and night?" Leslie asked

"That's a valid question," I replied. "I'm definitely not recommending that you don't pay your bills. The rate of bankruptcies in the U.S. is off the charts, and in many cases these people are simply wanting to walk away from their bills and their financial responsibilities. I do not support that at all. We made sure that all our bills were paid in full, and we were in constant communication with our creditors to make sure they understood they would be paid in full.

"The main point I'm making is that there is more than one way to deal with a financial problem. You have to be creative. Look at all your options. Make up – create – your options. Ask yourself, 'If I were to take on this pay-yourself-first program, how can I do it? What do I need to do differently?' Again, this habit was not about simply saving up some extra money. This was about building our financial future today. And I'll tell you, that money grew in those accounts faster than we ever expected."

"Explain again what those accounts were for," Leslie said.

I drew three boxes on a piece of paper:

INVESTING	CHARITY	SAVINGS

"First, we decided we needed to invest, so we set up an investing account. Second, we're big believers in the idea that you must give in order to receive so we set up a charity or tithing account. Third, we set up a general savings account as a cushion for real emergencies or special opportunities."

"The concept of 'pay yourself first' then isn't about treating yourself to a new pair of shoes or splurging on a trip to Tahiti. It's about taking care of yourself financially for the future," Leslie said thoughtfully.

"That's exactly what it is," I acknowledged. "And you bring up a great point because people do get confused about that and then go out and spend the money they've worked so hard to save on 'treats' for themselves… and end up back at zero. As a matter of fact the $5,000 down payment for my very first rental property – the little two-bedroom, one-bath house – was the first money to come out of our investing account."

"It's a little hard to imagine putting away 30 percent and living on only 70 percent of what I bring in," Leslie lamented.

"I guess if it was a piece of cake everyone would do it," I replied. "Be creative. Think about how you could do it. Better yet, think about this. Think about approximately how much money in total entered your home in the last year. Got it?"

"I got it," Leslie answered.

"Now take 30 percent of that figure and imagine how much more money would be sitting in your bank accounts today if you had started this exercise one year ago."

Leslie was smiling at the thought.

"So think about that. Think about what you will have instead of what you might have to let go of," I suggested.

Leslie looked puzzled. "Let go of?" she asked.

"Yes," I grinned. "Let go of. Like ways of doing things, that you've probably done forever, that you don't even realize you're doing, that are not getting you ahead."

"I get your point," she smiled.

"Do you still practice this habit today? Do you still take 30 percent off the top?" Tracey asked.

"We do. Except now the percentages are much larger than 30 percent. The only other difference today is that we're finding that the number-one thing we spend our savings on is our investments."

The three of us continued to talk. We all thoroughly enjoyed Leslie's choice of "restaurant," not to mention her delicious spread of food and drink. We savored every last morsel. We were in relaxation mode watching all the activity in the park when Leslie's cell phone rang…

EXERCISE:

1) What was the total amount of
   income that came into your
   household for the past 12 months? $_____

   If, for the past 12 months, you had
   put aside 30% of all monies that entered
   your home, then how much further
   ahead would you be today?
   Your 12-month income X .30 = $_____

2) What is your total monthly
   household income today? $_____

   Multiply your monthly household
   income by 12, for your future annual
   household income; $_____

   What other additional money can
   you expect to receive – tax refunds,
   gifts, investments, extra earned
   income, etc. $_____

   Total Household Income: $_____

   If, for the next 12 months, you
   put aside 30% of all monies that
   enter your home, then how much
   will you have accumulated to
   pay yourself first?

   Total Household Income X .30 = $_____

Chapter Fourteen

"MY PARTNER'S NOT INTERESTED!"

"Power is the ability not to have to please."
– *Elizabeth Janeway*

"Hello!" Leslie answered eagerly.

"Hi, Leslie, it's Pat!" the caller replied.

Leslie laughed. "Pat! I had a feeling this might be you. How great to have you join us for lunch… although we ate absolutely everything. Just a minute." Leslie put her cell phone on speaker. "Pat, say hi to Tracey and Kim."

"Hi! Glad to hear that Tracey made it. OK, now you've got to fill me in on everything you've been talking about."

Tracey jumped in. "I wish you were here with us. Thanks for calling in. I've actually been catching up with Kim and Leslie from your last get together. Leslie and I had been talking about your discussions on money and finances and investing, and I wanted to hear more, which is one of the reasons I'm here. It's been a great conversation. We miss you!"

"I wish I was there too," Pat responded. "Lots of *stuff* going on here. I know I'd have been better off being with you all."

Pat went on, "You know I shared with my husband some of our conversation from lunch at the Plaza – only the conversations about investing, not the parts about our single days. He just doesn't seem interested. His comment was, 'We make enough money. I don't think we need to risk it on investing. We'll be fine.' And that's as far as the conversation went. And that's as far as my efforts have gone as well. It's tough to start something new if your number-one partner isn't interested, and even more so when he's bringing home all the money. I'm not sure how to handle this."

We were quiet on the other end of the phone.

I thought to myself, "That's the million-dollar question. What do you do if your partner's not interested in investing and you are? How do you get started? Do you need his support? I know it's a lot easier if you have his support. And how do you come to agreement on the money to invest? This is not just about investing, this is about relationship… and that's a whole other area of psychosis." My head was spinning with thoughts.

I looked up and both Leslie and Tracey were staring at me as if to say, "What do you tell her? Tell her something. What should she do?"

I didn't know what to say. I had no personal experience with this sort of situation. Mine was just the opposite. I had a partner constantly pushing me to learn and to invest more and more. But looking back I have run into many, many women who have asked that same question. So I knew Pat was definitely not alone.

The first words that came out of my mouth were, "Pat, I do not have the answer for you. I wish I had the magic solution, but I think your question is one of the trickiest of all. It's not just about money. It's clearly also about your relationship. So let me think about it and let me talk with a few people, and I'll get back to you with what I discover. OK?"

"That would be great," Pat replied. "Thank you."

The four of us continued to talk. We decided to wrap it up just before the rush hour began. We gave hugs all around, including Pat via phone, and didn't know when we would see one another again but we all knew we'd stay in touch.

A Not Uncommon Issue

Pat's question stayed with me. What do you do if you want to start investing but your partner's not interested?

One trait I find in women, relating to this topic, is that most women will carefully and fully consider those around them when making changes or big decisions in their lives. Much more so then men. I believe this is why this question comes up so immediately for many women when they want to start investing. Women, in general, tend to include those around them in their decisions while men tend to have a more competitive, go-it-alone attitude.

My girlfriend came up with a great analogy around this very subject. She asked, "Have you ever watched kids at a pool party? If you ask a group of boys to line up along the side of the pool and all jump in together, here's what you'll see: They all line up and then it's every boy for himself, each attempting to outdo the other. Jack goes for the biggest splash. Charlie jumps the farthest. Pete does the best belly flop. And Danny stays under water the longest.

"Now ask the same thing of a group of girls, and what do they do? They all politely line up, hold hands and all jump in the pool on the count of three."

Now I have nothing against competition. I love competition. My point is that as women, in general, we tend to consider the feelings and thoughts of those close to us, as well as the impact on them, much more so than men. So it's natural that the question, "What if my partner's not interested in investing?" would come up often for women.

I've heard this question time and time again. (Just for the record, men do ask that question as well.) I just never had an answer to it. I am fortunate to have a partner in Robert who not only supports me with my investing but strongly (and I do mean strongly) encourages me to keep learning and to take on bigger challenges. He continually urges me to go beyond where I think I can go. So I personally don't have first-hand experience in this, yet I know many women, as well as men, are faced with this exact situation.

Four Options

As best I see it there are only four options for a woman with this dilemma. She can:

1) Invest with her partner as a team.
2) Invest on her own – with her partner's support.
3) Invest on her own – without her partner's support.
4) Don't invest.

Option #1 – This would be my ideal. As the saying goes, two heads are better than one. Investing involves an array of talents – from searching out the deal to negotiating the terms, to handling the fine print. Often couples who work as a team uncover talents they never knew they had and bring those talents into their investment strategy; and second, because they are both learning as they go they find they now have a lot to talk about. They make decisions together, study and learn together, and spend a great deal more time together. In the majority of cases this is great for the relationship as well as for investing success.

As one woman, Jasmine, wrote to me:

> My husband and I both felt that there had to be a better way to live life than as a slave to our corporate, high-stress jobs. We started by reading books together, which made a huge difference because both of our contexts (the big picture) were expanding at the same time. Reading, discussing the books, and exploring new ideas became a fun activity that we could do together, as well as deciding how we would divide up the major tasks in our real estate investing. As a woman, I like to know that I have a support structure; I don't necessarily need it, but I just like to know it's available to me.

Option #2 – This is the next best thing. If you have the support of your partner, then you're not fighting an uphill battle. He is on your side, and, I assume, wants you to win. I've actually spoken to many investors who start here. The husband said, "You go ahead. I support you but will not be actively involved."

What often happens is once you begin the process, and especially once he sees the money coming in, then it's hard to ignore. Instead of being a passive bystander, his interest level perks up, and he becomes more and more involved. As one woman yelled out at a talk I was doing when I asked what women do to get their uninterested husbands or partners interested in investing, "Show him the money!"

Here is a wonderful example from a gentleman whose wife was not interested. I include it because I think sometimes we women do not realize how much the men in our lives want us to be a bigger part of their lives.

> *I started on my own with her observing from the sidelines. I'd work all day, sometimes even working two jobs, then come home, have a quick bite to eat, and head out in search of my first cash flow property.*

> *After receiving a lot of "no's" I finally got a "yes" from a seller and quickly closed on a property that produced $350 a month cash flow. Believe me I wanted to give up a thousand times during that very first attempt, but sheer drive and determination drove me to continue. My wife joining me someday in this exciting enterprise was one of my biggest motivators.*

> *This continued on for a year. I'd come home after working all day and then work half the night on maintaining my properties. Having her help me in a more direct way would have certainly helped but I didn't bug her about it.*

> *Somewhere along the way she started getting excited. She saw my commitment, my sacrifice, and my belief in this investment vehicle... and she saw the money!*

> *It is a bit crazy raising two kids and managing 40-plus units and dealing with all that comes along with it. My wife is the best. I'm*

so very proud of what she's accomplished. It has been a path of personal development for both of us. We see the need to constantly grow and learn. I never could have imagined our relationship could be this amazing. There is nothing like it when you get it together... together.

Option #3 – This is not an easy position. You're not only stepping out into a whole new world, but you're doing so without the support of the number-one person in your life. So I won't pretend and say it's a piece of cake; it's not. Yet, over time, as with the gentleman above, once you have some success and viable results, your partner may turnaround and become your greatest supporter. It's women in this situation, and there are many of them, that more than ever depend upon the support from other people around them, ideally other investors.

This is where a women's investment group could prove invaluable, as can existing investment clubs and organizations. If you are in this situation, surround yourself with people with similar goals and ambitions as you have.

Option #4 – I hate to even include this as an option but in reality this is what many women opt to do – to not invest. As one woman told me,

"If my husband wasn't behind it then I fear it would be too hard on our marriage. I'm hoping eventually he'll come around." Unfortunately there is no quick fix or easy answer for getting a disinterested spouse or partner on board. However, the good news is that women are doing it all over the world.

How To Get Your Spouse/Partner On Board

In asking the question of investors, "How do you get your spouse interested in investing if he or she isn't interested?" I heard some very creative, as well as practical, approaches people took. Here are a few:

Megan

Megan was convinced that she wanted to get into the game of investing. She had been dancing around the idea for two years, and the time had come for her to make the move. She sat down with her husband, Jeff, and explained what she wanted to do and that she wanted him to be a part of it.

His response was, "I don't have time for this. My work takes up all my time. This seems very important to you so you go ahead. Keep me informed of what you're doing."

She was disappointed he didn't share in her enthusiasm but the fact that he at least wanted to hear what she was doing was some consolation.

Megan's interest was rental properties. After about four months of researching different areas and learning about the market, Megan found exactly the type of rental house she was looking for. As she looked at it from the curb, an idea struck her of how to get her husband involved in her first property.

The next Sunday, she suggested they go out to breakfast at "this restaurant that I hear is very good." That restaurant was conveniently about six blocks from her targeted property. Jeff was a graphic designer. He was very creative and artistic. So Megan slowly drove by her house and stopped in front of it and asked, "Jeff, if this was your property what would you do to fix it up?"

Jeff said, "First you've got to clean up the yard. The walkway could be stepping-stones with grass in between. Contemporary awnings and a warmer paint color would give the house a more welcoming feel. And I'd definitely replace the front door."

"Do you want to do that with me?" she smiled.

"What are you talking about?" he said and then it clicked. "This is the property you want to buy, isn't it?"

I believe the two most heated subjects in the world are relationships and money. So when you put the two together, anything can happen.

It's no wonder that the number-one subject couples fight about today is – can you guess? Money.

On that day Megan and Jeff became real estate investment partners. Megan cleverly recognized how to spark Jeff's interest by bringing his true talents into play. As long as Megan talked about the numbers and dealing with brokers Jeff couldn't care less. But when he looked at the property through an artist's eyes he had a personal interest in the project.

When I mentioned this story to another woman with a disinterested partner, she said, "That's perfect! My partner loves to garden. He comments on every yard in our neighborhood about how he could do it better. Now he can!"

Edwin

Edwin wrote:

> *How I got my wife and kids interested was simply by getting them involved. We played the CASHFLOW 101 board game regularly as a family so the kids learned right along with us. On weekends we would do our drive-bys to look for properties in our mini-van. We played the game "The Price Is Right" – guessing the actual square footage, number of bedrooms and baths, and the price – then we'd pick up the flyer and compete to see who was closer. In other words, we created games and made it fun for everyone involved.*

Leia

Leia was a bit crafty in her approach:

> *When my dad gave me a copy of* Retire Young Retire Rich *I devoured it. That's what I wanted – to be financially free. I tried to give my husband the Cliff Notes version each night (he's not an avid reader), but it wasn't making sense to him.*

> *I mentioned this problem to my friend. Knowing we were going on a six-hour car trip that weekend, he lent me his copy of* Rich Dad Poor Dad *on audio CD. My husband, being trapped in the car with me for six hours and being a more auditory learner, had no choice but to listen.*

And an amazing thing happened… epiphany! It suddenly all clicked. We had great conversations the rest of the trip about these ideas and how we could change our lives. We've now started our investment business and just purchased an investment property.

Andrea

Andrea took the ultimate plunge. She said:

My husband was a high-flying stockbroker in Kuala Lumpur, Malaysia. In 1998, after the Asian financial crisis, he lost his business, and we lost more than half our net worth in the stock market.

We moved to the U.S. My husband went back into the financial services industry, and he plowed what we had left into the stock market (again!). I started a small business from home. In 2000 our portfolio was up by 60 percent and I urged him to sell. Of course he would not listen to the "little wife." He said we were in for the "long term." Being a good wife who let the husband be the captain of the ship, I did not insist. Two weeks later the market crashed. Our life savings were almost completely wiped out.

Then came September 11, 2001, and both of our businesses ran out of steam. We had a large mortgage, no savings left, and we were out of options. You can imagine the tension and the resentment in our household. It was not healthy for our children or for us.

Finally I came to grips with my own feelings of fear, anger, and resentment. Like many women, I gave away my power to my husband because he was the primary breadwinner. I asked my husband to listen to me for once and to treat me as an equal partner in all aspects of our lives, including financial. I asked him to stop getting defensive and angry whenever we discussed money. I asked that we work together as a team and for him to stop fighting and ridiculing my ideas. I gave him an ultimatum – either he come to the table as my partner and work together to get us out of our financial mess or we go our separate ways. I took a huge chance, knowing the consequences to our lives, especially the consequences for our children.

Thankfully my gamble paid off. Finally we were a team, working together for the benefit of our family. I was no longer the "little wife" but a valid working partner in this marriage. Today, we've turned it all around. We have eight rental condos in Waikiki, and we completed two property development projects. In two years we anticipate we will be out of the rat race and financially free.

I know it's not easy to achieve financial freedom if your partner is not on your side, and I sure hope it does not take the threat of a divorce for your partner to wake up.

One More Thought

In hearing from numerous people on this topic there were two consistent suggestions that came up again and again. The first was: wherever possible include your spouse or partner in the process. Whatever investment vehicle you decide to pursue, gently involve your partner in what you're doing and learning. At first it may be just pointing out an applicable article in the paper or talking about a speaker you heard discussing the trends in your local real estate market. Many people stated they were successful in turning their partners' interest around by including, not excluding, them throughout the process. More communication, not less, was the key for many couples.

The second recommendation was for women to take the first step; take the initiative. One woman said, "I knew it was up to me to get things started. I trusted my husband would come around. Eventually he did. He saw how dedicated and enthusiastic I was, which got his attention. And when he saw the money he was hooked!"

Your Relationship In Relation To Money

All these stories bring up an important question that I think most couples should address. The question is,

"What is the quality of your relationship in relation to money?"

In other words, do you openly discuss your money situation with one another? Does one person in your relationship generally make the financial decisions? Do you discuss and make these decisions together? Is money a subject the two of you rarely, if ever, discuss?

The reason for the question is that I believe the two most heated subjects in the world are relationships and money. So when you put the two together, anything can happen. It's no wonder that the number-one subject couples fight about today is – can you guess? Money.

"Do You Want To Be Rich?"

Robert asked me very early on in our relationship this question: "Do you have any problem with being very rich?" I thought to myself, "What a strange question. Who would have a problem with that?"

I said to Robert, "I would definitely have no problem with that. Why would you ask?"

He said, "You'd be surprised at how many women I've come across that find it offensive to be focused on making a lot of money. Or they think that it's superficial to have a goal to be rich. There are plenty of people out there who think that money isn't a subject to be discussed openly. It's amazing that money, something every one of us uses every single day of the year, would be taboo to talk about. I never understood that. As my Rich Dad said, 'Money may not be the most important thing in your life, but it affects everything that is important.' It affects the level of healthcare you receive, your and your kid's education, food, shelter, etc. Why people don't discuss it is beyond me. I plan on being very rich, so I want to know how your feel about it. That's why I asked the question."

From there we talked a lot more on the subject. We shared the type of lifestyle we each wanted. We discussed whether or not money was talked about in our families growing up. What were we each told about money when we were kids? Often the behavior in your family related to money will carry forward into your adult relationships. What did money represent to each of us?

It was a fascinating conversation – one that I had never had before with anyone. Many of the points we discussed I had never even thought about previously. It was very refreshing, candid, and, of course, it raised so many questions in my head.

The point is that we each had an understanding of where one another stood on the subject of money. It also gave us permission to talk openly with each other about everything related to money. The mysterious veil that often clouds the subject had been lifted.

How To Talk About Money

If money isn't something you talk about candidly and openly, then you may want to make a special date with your partner and begin the conversation. Here are a few questions the two of you could answer to get you started:

> – What did your parents tell you about the subject of money?
> – Did your own thoughts differ from those of your parents?
> – What does money represent to you?
> – What's your general thought about very rich people?
> – How rich is "very rich"?

Many people are not comfortable talking about money for one reason or another, so if you get some immediate resistance from your partner once you broach the subject just take it slow and gentle. It's no different than bringing up any subject that may be uncomfortable. You simply work it from several angles until you find the one that gets the response. I've found that once I get that initial foot in the door then the rest flows pretty naturally.

Back To Pat

I called Pat to pick up where we left off on our last phone call. We talked about how she and her husband handle money in their marriage. It was not a big surprise to find out that the subject is rarely discussed. He makes the money, and she pays the bills. That's about as far as it goes. They talk about large financial purchases such as their home, cars, and vacations. All the investing is done by her husband, which amounts to purchasing some mutual funds and occasionally a stock buy that his stockbroker recommends. Other than that the subject of money is a non-subject in Pat's household.

"This may be my best moment as a journalist; to get my husband to actually open up and talk about money," Pat declared. "This will take kid gloves but it's a great place to start."

I shared with Pat a few of the stories from investors who started just like her. She was silent as I read them. I could hear the wheels in her head turning.

"Thanks for sharing those with me. The pieces are already starting to fall into place. I have to say, it's really good to know that there are other women in my same situation and that they took action and did something about it. I was beginning to feel trapped. Now I can see some options. My biggest concern was that this was going to cause a serious rift in my marriage, and it was worrying me. Hearing from other women tells me it's doable, that there are solutions. That I can take control now and not wait and hope that my husband will come around. My ideal scenario will be that my husband participates in this with me, since I think that will give us a common goal and make our marriage stronger. And if he chooses not to, I can't let that stop me. I'll let you know how it goes!" Pat said enthusiastically.

The tone in Pat's voice was alive. "I wish you all the best!" I said. "I do know you, Pat, and once you set your mind to it, you do tend to get what you want. Bye!"

As we hung up, this fleeting thought passed by: I wasn't worried about Pat any more. She would be just fine. It was Pat's husband I was feeling a little nervous for. His life was about to change.

Chapter Fifteen

WHY WOMEN MAKE GREAT INVESTORS

"We women don't care too much about getting our pictures on money as long as we can get our hands on it."
– Ivy Baker Priest,
U.S. Treasurer, 1954

It's time to once and for all break away from those old female stereotypes with which many of us have been raised. We can buy into the myth that women and investing do not mix. (Or as one unaware man replied when I told him I was writing a book on women and investing, "Women and investing, that's an oxymoron! Women and *spending*, yes. But not women and investing." Can you believe that? I chose not to reply. I was taught to choose my battles wisely. This guy was anything but wise.)

We can pretend not to be smart. We can pretend to be silly and confused when it comes to finance. We can play the role of the woman behind the man (be it your boss, your husband, even your business partner). It's a stereotype with which we women have been living and often fighting against for eons.

The bottom line is we are smart. Truth be told, we know more than we ever let on. Plus we have uncanny common sense. Not to mention priceless intuition. The fact that money, investing, and finance have not been the role of women in the past... so what?

Times have changed. Times continue to change. Times always change.

It's no longer a valid excuse to say, "I'm not good with money," or

"I don't know anything about investing." The past doesn't matter at this point. What does matter is the choice you make today.

It's Your Choice

As best I see it there are two choices: 1) Accept that you have no place in the world of money and investing – be content in balancing a checkbook and paying the family bills. OR 2) Choose to take control of your financial life. Know that your financial future is up to you and no one else. Get smart with your money. Get prepared. Take action. And go make things happen.

It truly is decision time. (And many of you have already made your decision.) You can talk about it all you want. Think about it forever. Research the topic until you're blue in the face. But there comes a point when you need to make a conscious decision one way or the other. I suggest that that point in time be now.

This is the decision: Am I going to commit to do what it takes for my personal financial success... or not? If not, then I understand that I am agreeing to allow someone else to be responsible for my financial well-being... and accept the consequences that go along with that. If, on the other hand, I am willing to commit, then it's time to put aside all excuses and get to work. Very simply, that is the decision facing you.

The choice is yours.

Moving To Your Future

Up to this point we've talked about the objections, the thoughts, and the misinformation that has paralyzed many of us when it comes to putting our toes in the investment waters. Now it's time to move into the future. How do you become an incredibly successful investor? If you're just starting out, where do you begin? If you're already an investor, how do you become even more successful? That's what the rest of this book is about.

The Good News

Let's begin with the good news. The good news is that women

make great investors. The statistics prove it. The women investors I've met throughout the world prove it. And more and more women are proving it every day.

The statistics have shown time and time again that women are natural investors. Here are a few facts:

- A 2000 National Association of Investors Corporation (NAIC) study found that women-only clubs achieved average annual returns of 32% since 1951 vs 23% for men-only investment clubs.

- A study of investment behavior by Terrance Odean, professor at the University of California-Davis, found that women actually get better returns than men – 1.4 percentage points better.

- A 1995 NAIC study revealed that women-only investment clubs out-performed men-only investment clubs in 9 of the past 15 years.

- A study done by Merrill Lynch Investment Managers found the following investment behaviors among men and women:

	Women	Men
Hold onto a losing investment for too long	35%	47%
Wait too long to sell a strong investment	28%	43%
Buy a hot investment without researching it first	13%	24%
Make the same investment mistake more than once	47%	63%

The verdict is in – women do know how to handle money.

Women vs. Men

There are countless articles written about who is better at investing – men or women. I don't subscribe to the idea that, as a whole, one gender is better at investing than the other. It's not a gender thing. Just as there are great singers and not-so-great singers. Just as there are brilliant chefs and lousy chefs. Just as there are hugely successful business people and dismal failures. There are winning investors and losing investors. It's about the individual. It's about her or his skills, her or his knowledge, and her or his experience that makes the difference between profits and losses in the world of investing.

Having said that, there do seem to be some definite advantages many of us have, as women, as we approach the world of investing. There are many things that we do very well, some even naturally, that are particularly applicable to being a great investor. Now, I realize not every single woman will have these traits, yet I think many of us will see ourselves in most of them. And it's our job to use them to our benefit.

The Eight Advantages That Make Women Great Investors

1) We're Not Afraid To Say, "I Don't Know"

I would say, by far, the number-one advantage most women have when it comes to investing is that we are not afraid to say the words, "I don't know." We are more willing to ask questions and admit when we don't understand something. The person who has to know all the answers, who's afraid of looking stupid, never learns or grows. If you have to appear to know everything and never let on when you don't know something, then you'll never ask the questions to find out more. You'll stop learning. It's those who are afraid of looking stupid who actually are stupid.

My friend Frank is 85 years old. He is one of the most brilliant investors and businesspeople I know. One thing I love about him is that he has the curiosity of a 7-year-old. He is interested in everything and is always asking questions. One day I was with Frank. We were introduced to a man about 35 years old.

Frank asked, "What type of business are you in?"

The man replied, "I work on Wall Street. I work with companies who want to go public."

Frank said, "That must be fascinating! Tell me more." And this gentleman spoke to Frank for the next 20 minutes telling him all about taking companies public. Frank didn't say a word. He just listened curiously. As we walked away Frank turned to me and said, "That was pretty interesting."

Now the beauty of this story is that Frank began on Wall Street in his 20s. He has taken many, many companies public. He still does that today. He has a wealth of knowledge in this arena, yet he still takes the time to listen to what a rookie has to say because he may learn something new. Frank is a wonderful role model. He never comes across as a know-it-all and because of that he knows a lot.

The advantage we women have in being confident enough to say, "I don't know" is that it opens up the doors for us to learn so many answers. The answers may come from asking in conversation, "Would you explain that to me? I'm not familiar with that." Or maybe you read an article or hear something on TV that sounds intriguing, but you don't fully comprehend it, then you might go online or go to the library to research it.

I truly believe that having the confidence to say, "I don't know" is one of the most powerful learning tools we, as women, have. And it does take confidence. Pretending to know all the answers because you don't want to look stupid comes from low confidence or low self-esteem. So stand up and be proud to admit, "I don't know!" You'll be amazed at how much you will know.

2) We're Willing To Ask For Help

Piggybacking on #1, the second advantage a lot of us have is that we are much more willing to ask for help than men are.

I was visiting my friends Marie and Carl, a married couple, at their house one afternoon. Carl was busy in the guest bathroom, tools spread everywhere, tinkering with the toilet. Marie walked by

Ask yourself: Am I going to commit to do what it takes for my personal financial success... or not? That's the decision.

and innocently asked, "Carl, why don't I call the plumber and ask him what the problem might be?"

"No need for that," Carl replied. "I'll have it fixed in just a minute."

One hour later Carl appeared from the bathroom, looking tired and frustrated, and said to Marie, "I think you should call the plumber. The problem is bigger than I thought."

The plumber came over and ended up replacing the entire toilet. Carl's comment of course was, "See, I told you it was a big problem." Later, behind the scenes, the plumber, a friend of this couple, told Marie that the actual original cause of the problem was one small piece that he could have easily replaced, but because of all of Carl's tinkering, the toilet was beyond repair.

Marie's first instinct was to call the plumber and ask for help. It's no different than the common scenario of the couple lost in the back roads of an unfamiliar town and the woman suggests they stop and ask directions. The man refuses, saying, "I'll figure out where we are. I'm sure we're on the right track." When it comes to investing, women will ask for directions. They will ask for help. There are two advantages here: first, they will learn something new; second, they will not waste their time figuring it out on their own.

3) Women Are Great Shoppers

Most women are great shoppers. Why does that matter? Because they know how to spot a bargain. The formula for bargain shopping is the same for investing – look for something that is priced below its actual value and buy it.

> *Ruth Hayden, financial educator and author said it best: "If we women shopped (investments) the way we shopped Nordstrom's, we'd be in the money. When stocks are low, it's like a three-for-one panty sale."*

Women who are shoppers know the value of a Louis Vuitton purse or a pair of Donna Karan jeans. They are very familiar with the product, so they know when they see a good deal. It's no different when it comes to investing. If you are familiar with and paying attention to certain stocks or to a particular neighborhood for rental property, then you'll see the good deals when they appear. If you're not familiar with the "products" and have not spent any time checking out the prices, then you'll have no idea what the real value of the product or investment is. The formula is the same. Find a quality item on sale and buy it. Simple.

4) Women Do Their Homework

Women, as a general rule, do their homework. Women do not typically buy off a "hot tip." According to the National Center for Women and Retirement Research (NCWRR), women spend more time researching their investment choices than men do. This prevents women from trading on whims and going after the "hot tips" – behavior that tends to weaken men's portfolios.

Women tend not to be big point-of-purchase buyers. Instead they buy because the deal makes sense.

5) Women Are Risk-Averse

Following on the heels of #4, studies have shown women to be "risk-averse" as compared to men. I've heard arguments that the reason women will not be successful as investors is because they are less willing to take risks. If it is true that women are less prone to take risks, then is that such a bad thing?

I know for me, whenever I venture into an investment that I feel is a bit more risky or unfamiliar to me I tend to study it a little more than usual and do my homework with a little more effort before laying out a lot of money. If women truly are risk-averse, then this may lead them to do a little more research on the investments they are pursuing, which leads them to greater success with their investments – as the statistics prove.

The one trap, women, we need to watch out for is when our aversion to risk keeps us in constant analysis and research. This is commonly referred to as analysis paralysis. If this happens, then we may end up doing nothing. Use risk to your advantage. Don't let it paralyze you.

6) Women Have Much Less Ego

I'm sure I'll get some feedback from the men on this one.

Women have much less ego when it comes to their investments. My girlfriend investors tend to be very practical, matter-of-fact, and very conscious of the return on their investments. It's no secret men can tend to display a bit (or is it a lot?) of ego or bravado when showing off their investments. The only thing my girlfriends want to show is the money. Show me the money! Or as Ivy Baker Priest, U.S. Treasurer in 1954 said,

> *"We women don't care too much about getting our pictures on money as long as we can get our hands on it."*

Mika Hamilton of the Global Investment Institute writes:

> *Being involved with a company that trains people how to actively trade in the stock market I have seen thousands of both men and women start off down the road to prosperity through various types of investing. Approximately 80 percent of our clients are male. But I'd wager that 80 percent of the most successful investors are women.*

> *Based on this experience, I began to wonder why it is that women tend to be better investors than men. I thought about it over and over, and I could not ignore the facts. Women make more successful investors than men.*

> *But why? I think it comes down to three simple words: EGO, EGO, EGO. The one thing that most men have in common is a macho ego.*

> *Men tend to let their egos make their decisions for them. They hold*

when they should sell. They buy-in for fear of missing out on that one big opportunity. They refuse to ask questions or to ask for help in fear of looking silly.

In other words men are more interested in looking strong, knowledgeable, or successful. They invest not to get the best deal out of the market but invest so that they look good (or not look bad).

Women on the other hand, are much more likely to ask questions until they fully understand what they are learning, and they are usually more interested in the goal, (in this case making money) than they are in impressing the people around them.

Usually when people think of investing, they think of taking chances and risks. But the truth is that investing has much more to do with emotional intelligence than most people realize. Emotional intelligence is the ability to think objectively about a situation and not get too emotionally involved in it. Women, in general, possess a high emotional intelligence.

This quality makes women great investors. Rather than investing according to what will make them look good, women will invest according to a plan – not according to what mood they are in or whether they will be "right" or "wrong."

7) Women Are Nurturers

When it comes to investing women tend to nurture their investments. I was talking with an investor the other day about one of her apartment buildings. She proudly talked about how she had fixed it up and improved the look and feel of the property. She mentioned what wonderful tenants she had and that she made a point to meet each one of them. She took care of her property and her tenants. She nurtured them. In return her tenants recommended the apartments to their friends. Her property was fully occupied with a waiting list, and because of that she was able to keep her rents comparatively high. Because of her high occupancy and strong rents the value of her property continues to increase.

Part of the nurturing process involves establishing good relationships with her investment network. This may include business/stock/real estate brokers, finance lenders, investors, members of clubs and organizations, tenants, individuals privy to information on future progress within her city, tax professionals, and mentors – just to name a few. The stronger her relationships the better the information she receives, which can be invaluable when building an investment portfolio.

8) Women Learn Well From Other Women
This is why there is growing popularity among all-women investment clubs. These clubs are popping up all over the world, and they are a great way to get introduced to, or to learn more about, the world of investing.

Women share with one another. If they find something that works they want to share it with their friends. This may be why the women-only investment clubs out-perform the all-men clubs. Women typically want their friends to succeed.

The downside of this is that women may sometimes take information from women who have no experience. They'll listen to advice because, "she's my friend." Please be sure that the women to whom you are talking about investing are like-minded and have similar investing goals. Otherwise you may be wasting a lot of your time.

For example my friend Michelle came to me and said she wanted to buy a rental property in Phoenix. Over several days we looked at many properties. We came across a townhouse in a resort community, surrounded by trees and overlooking the pool. It was one of the best locations in the entire complex. After collecting the rent and paying the expenses and the mortgage she was going to put $250.00 per month in her pocket. It was the perfect first investment property. An agreement was reached between her and the seller, and she began her inspection and due-diligence period. I then left for a one-month trip overseas.

When I returned I called Michelle and asked, "When do you close on your first rental property?"

There was a moment of silence, and then she said, "I decided not to go through with it."

I took a deep breath and, somewhat frustrated, asked, "Why didn't you go through with it? It seemed like a great property for you."

She explained, "After you left I went and talked to my friend Candace. I told her all about the property, and she told me that it was a very risky investment."

"Why did she say it was risky?" I asked.

"She told me that her friend had a rental property, and she couldn't find a tenant, and she lost money on it. So she said she wouldn't buy it if it was her decision," Michelle explained.

After much silence I had to ask, "Has your friend Candace ever owned a rental property?"

"No," Michelle replied.

"So why would you take advice about an investment she knows absolutely nothing about?" I asked in a raised voice. "That's like asking a vegetarian to recommend a great steak house. If you're going to ask someone for advice, make sure you ask someone who knows what she's talking about. Someone who has actually done what you're going to do!"

Yes, women do learn from other women. Just be sure that the women you're learning from have done, or are doing, what it is you want to do.

This is why I like the women-only investment clubs. Most of the women in these clubs are like-minded and have an aligned goal – to make money from their investments. The investment clubs generally fall into two categories: 1) educational and 2) resource pooling. As I said earlier, I strongly support the clubs that are pure education – where women study and learn together. They share with each other the investments they own and the ones they are pursuing, as well as what they've learned along the way.

I'm a bit wary of clubs whose members pool their money and buy an investment as a group. The reason is that unless each member is crystal clear on the agreements and the agreements are all in writing, there can be plenty of room for disappointment and upset. I prefer to separate the education from the actual investing.

We Can Do This… We Already Are

There is no great secret about how to invest. That's the easy part. The key for most women is making the shift in mindset from "I can't" or "I don't know how" to "Not only can I be an investor, I can be a great investor!"

There is one little secret I will share with you – once you get into the investing game… it's fun. The inspiring and excited comments I hear time and time again from women investors are, "I don't know what I was so scared about. I'm loving this!" "I don't know why I didn't start sooner!" "It is so fun making money!" "I can't wait until my next deal!" "I'm learning so much!"

Is it becoming clear to you? Women make fabulous investors! We are cut out for this. More and more women today are becoming investors… and proving that we're more than good at it. And proving that it's fun. It's fun to make money. It's fun to learn and grow. It's fun to feel a newfound self-esteem. Most importantly, it's fun to know that we're in control of our lives – and because of that more choices and opportunities are available to us. That is a powerful and freeing position in which to be.

Chapter Sixteen

"I'M READY TO START!"

"Thoughts are energy, and you can make your world or break your world by your thinking."

- Susan Taylor

The one person I hadn't connected with from our original group in Hawaii was Martha. I wanted to touch base with her and see how she was doing.

"Hi, this is Martha," she answered when I called.

"Hi, Martha. It's Kim. A voice from your Hawaii past."

"It's so good to hear from you. I'm really sorry I couldn't make the reunion. I spoke with Pat and Leslie. Things have been so busy. I wanted to call when you guys had your lunch in the park but something came up," she apologized.

"No problem," I said. "Do you have a few minutes to catch up?"

Martha hesitated for a moment then said, "Sure. Now is a good time."

"Since you and I haven't spoken, I just wanted to say hi and catch up with you. It's been a long time," I started.

There was silence. "Martha? Are you there?" I asked.

"OK. Here it is," she said determinedly. "I've been very reluctant to get together with all of you because things aren't very happy for me right now. To be honest my life is nothing like

There is no magic formula for investing... no secret pill that promises that in two days you will become instant successful investors. Investing is a process and it takes 'doing our homework' and lots of legwork to become savvy investors.

what I envisioned it would be when we were all in Hawaii. Pat shared some of your stories with me, and, to be honest, I'm embarrassed at where I am today," she admitted. "Remember how I wanted to be a world-class oceanographer?"

"I remember it well," I answered.

"Well, about two years into it my dad called and said he needed help with the family business. His top employee left, and he was in a bind. He said it would just be for a couple of months until he brought a new person on board. I grew up in the business so I knew it well, but business, in general, was not something I was interested in. So, out of obligation, I left my work in Hawaii, and I went back home to help out for a few months. I don't know what happened but a few months turned into a year and then three years, and here I am still today. My dad sold the business about seven years ago, but he didn't get a lot of money. It was a comfortable life for my mom and dad, but my father became ill shortly after he sold his business, and a large amount of their savings went toward his medical care. He since passed away. I'm working two jobs just to keep my head above water."

"Pat said your mom was ill. Is she alright?"

"Yes, she's OK now. But since she didn't have much money left after Dad's death, she has moved in with me since I'm the only child. That's why I'm working two jobs, to support the both of us. As she gets older her health has been a bit of a problem. We have insurance, but it never seems to cover all the needs. So it's been a rough few years.

"What surprises me most is that at first I became so complacent with my life. After I moved back to San Diego everything was easy. I didn't have to struggle to pay the rent. I had money from the business. I had a car, and my apartment was two blocks from the beach. I could surf when I wanted. It was all very comfortable. I guess that's why I stayed. It was easy."

She continued. "But I've discovered two major problems with the 'easy life.' First, I always wonder what would have happened had I pursued my oceanography. I have some regret there. And second, it seems that the easy life has now become the hard life. I always lived day to day – surfed whenever I could, spent every penny I made on play and party – but now those moments are behind me, and I've got to face the future, which right now looks like one big struggle.

So I apologize. That's why I haven't wanted to get together with everyone. I'm really struggling, and I'm not much fun to be around. "

"I can understand how you feel, and I trust our friendship goes deeper than that," I reassured her.

"Thank you," she said. "I'm just not sure where to go from here."

Martha sounded pretty desperate, so I took a chance. "Let me ask you this. Are you willing to make some changes to begin to pull yourself out of this?"

"Absolutely. Something has to change. I can't continue on like this. I just don't see any light at the end of the tunnel," she replied.

"If I were to send you a book, would you read it?" I asked.

"Of course I would."

"Then I'll send it, and after you read it, call me and we'll talk about it." I kept on. "I'm not saying this is the answer for you, but if the information sparks some interest, then at least it's a start."

"I will read it," she said emphatically. "I'll start as soon as I receive it."

With that we hung up. I sent Martha a copy of *Rich Dad Poor Dad* and waited to hear back from her.

"I'm Ready"

About one month later it dawned on me that I never heard back from Martha. I thought about calling her but decided that if she really wanted to turn her life around she was going to have to make that first step. I couldn't do it for her.

Just then my cell phone rang. It was Leslie calling. She was very excited. "OK, I'm ready!" she exclaimed

"Ready for what?" I asked.

"Ready to learn what I need to learn and do what I need to do to get myself financially set for life," she declared. "I'm fed up with just getting by. I've had enough. I'm ready to take action. And this is not just talk. I really mean it."

"I can tell," I replied. "What caused this sudden, urgent desire?"

"Months ago," Leslie started, "I signed up for a two-day art class in Vermont. It was a landscape class where we were outside with our easels in the beautiful Vermont countryside, which is my absolutely most favorite thing to do. I made all the arrangements and chose a date in fall when all the leaves were in brilliant color. I was so excited about this trip. The day before my boss at the art gallery called and said they had an opportunity to host a showing for a well-known artist and I had to be there for it. They never said it but I could hear in my boss' voice that it was either come into work tomorrow or don't come back."

"So what did you do?" I asked

She continued. "I felt as if I had no choice. I had to go into work for the showing. So I cancelled my Vermont plans, and I was in the gallery the next day. Now, I realize that emergencies come up and plans have to be changed, but in that instant it struck me what little control I have over my life. And it's all because of money. It was one of those 'aha' moments. The lights went on for me, and I don't want to go backward. It's time for me to move forward."

"Wow. I'm excited for you," I said. "It sounds like having to cancel your art trip was actually the best thing that could have happened to you. It got you off your you-know-what."

"Yeah, I guess it did," she said thinking through it.

"So what are you going to do?" I asked.

She jumped right in. "Here is my idea. Hear me out. Keep an open mind, and you tell me if you're willing."

"Am I sure I want to hear this idea of yours?" I asked tentatively.

"I hope so. Here it is," she said excitedly. "We set aside two full days. We invite the women from our Hawaii group. We fly to Phoenix. And we spend two days with you, and you share with us the steps you took to get started… and to keep growing your investments. What do you think?"

This time I was silent. "Look, I just keep learning as I go. I certainly don't have all the answers. And I don't follow the traditional investment strategies that most financial 'experts' preach. I've learned from some brilliant people, and today I have very smart people around me from whom I learn every day when it comes to my investments."

Leslie interrupted. "I understand that. I want to learn your strategy and then keep learning. From what I've heard so far it makes perfect sense to me. And as far as the people around you today, those people weren't there when you started. You said you started with nothing. And that's where I am today. I have nothing... except a strong desire to learn and to start making things happen. So, looking back, what did you do? How did you take your first steps? You said that women learn well from other women so I figure if we get the group together we'll learn a lot. And it's an environment where we won't be intimated to ask questions. Not like some of the investment meetings I've attended where the only people that ask questions are those who want to show off how smart they are. This way we would all learn from each other."

I laughed. "And you once told me you weren't a good salesperson. That was one persuasive sales pitch."

"Are you saying yes?" she prodded.

"Yes, but only under two conditions," I explained. "First, the two days are open only to the women who really want to learn. If they're just coming to hang out with their friends, then it's best they don't come. The desire to learn, and more importantly, to take action has to come from inside them. You cannot talk them into it."

"That's a good point. I'll just put out the invitations and see who shows up," she agreed. "And second?"

"Second, whoever shows up is crystal clear that there is no magic formula. I do not have the secret pill that promises that in two days you will become instant successful investors. Everyone must understand that investing is a process, and they will need to do their homework and the legwork to become savvy investors. I don't want them showing up with unrealistic expectations. Would you be sure to make them aware of that?"

"Done. Can we set a date?" Leslie pressed.

I smiled. "Yes, we can Miss I-don't-know-how-to-sell. Yeah right!"

I told Leslie about my conversation with Martha. I asked her to invite her as well. "It's funny," I said. "I was just thinking about her when you called. I sent her the book over a month ago, and I haven't heard a word from her."

Chapter Seventeen

NINETY PERCENT OF SUCCESS IS JUST SHOWING UP!

*"Just trying to do something – just being there, showing up –
is how we get braver. Self-esteem is about doing."*
– Joy Browne

Woody Allen once said, "Ninety percent of success is just showing up." I believe there is a lot of truth in that statement. Many people say they want to lose weight, but who actually shows up at the gym? Some say they want to do more for their community, but who shows up at the town council meetings? A lot of us say we want to do things to improve our lives, but what do we actually show up to?

That being said I was anxious to see who would show up for our two day investment session. Leslie was organizing everything, and she told each woman if they wanted to attend to meet at my house Friday morning at 9:00 a.m. "They all said they wanted to be there," she reported to me.

"We'll just see who shows up," I told her.

9:00 A.M. Friday

Coffee was on. Leslie arrived at 8:30 with fruit and an assortment of muffins. "I didn't pressure anyone," she promised me. "I simply told them what we'd be doing. I sent everyone directions. And I said there's no need to call me back, just show up if this was important to them."

"And you got a positive response from everyone?" I asked

"I did! Everyone. Even Martha. They all said how much they wanted to be part of this."

I poured two cups of coffee and she and I talked. At a few minutes to 9:00 the doorbell rang. We both looked at each other with excitement, like two kids about to lock ourselves into the front car of a roller coaster, knowing it would be quite a ride and wondering who would be coming along. We hurried to the front door and opened it.

"Hi! Great directions, Leslie! The taxi driver knew exactly where to go. I'm so glad to be here!" Tracey said a bit out of breath.

"Tracey, it's great to have you here!" I said with enthusiasm.

"You act as if you're surprised to see me," she said. "You didn't think I'd show up? There was no question in my mind, especially after what happened last week."

We walked toward the kitchen. "What happened?" I asked.

"Remember I told you the fear I faced when we worried that my husband would be fired when his company was sold?" she reminded us.

We both nodded.

"Last Friday the company made this major announcement," she began.

"There had been talk for about a year about our company merging with another but last we heard that had all fallen through. So, Friday afternoon the CEO called us all together and announced that the merger did in fact not happen, but instead our company was sold to our biggest competitor! The CEO was upfront with us that there would be changes and did his best to assure us that no job cuts had been announced. But how can we not be unnerved by all this?"

Many people say they want to lose weight, but who actually shows up at the gym?

Some say they want to do more for their community, but who shows up at the town council meetings?

A lot of us say we want to do things to improve our lives, but what do we actually show up to?

"What do you think is going to happen?" Leslie asked.

"I don't know, but I'll tell you, last week was like working in a morgue. Of course there are going to be job cuts. That's how buyouts work! Everyone is walking around in fear of losing their jobs. It's horrible. And on top of that, because no one, from the top down, knows what the future holds, no decisions are being made. It's like everyone's lives are on hold. It's so depressing. So I'm not sure what I'm going to do yet but your timing for these two days is perfect. This is the only thing I feel I have some control over. Heaven knows I have none in my job.

"Whew! Nothing like a wake-up call!" Leslie proclaimed.

"Is someone knocking on the door?" Tracey asked.

We were so busy talking that we didn't hear the doorknocker banging against the front door.

"Let's see whose behind door number two," I laughed.

All three of us walked down the hallway to see who it was. We were all guessing who we thought it would be. I opened the door.

"I can't believe I'm 10 minutes late! I had everything planned down to the minute. I'm never late," Pat said apologetically.

"C'mon in, Pat!" I said. We all hugged and headed back to the kitchen.

We talked over coffee, fruit, and muffins until about 9:45 and came to the conclusion that this was the group. No one else was showing up.

What Happened To Martha?

I later discovered what happened with Martha. Martha, you recall, was the one who was desperate to do *whatever it took* to change her situation. Who promised to read the book I sent her. She was the only one, Leslie later admitted, who said she would *definitely* be at our two-day gathering. It turned out she had never got to page one of *Rich Dad Poor Dad*. She never took one step to do anything different from what she was doing. I'm sure she had no intention of being with us for these two days. Martha was a lot of talk but zero action. She wanted her life to change but she wasn't willing to do anything different. She wasn't willing to change. Period. That's why I find that it's so important to only work with people who truly want what I have to offer - who truly want to learn. Otherwise it's like one of my favorite sayings:

> *Don't teach pigs to sing.*
> *It wastes your time... and it annoys the pig.*

There are a lot of people who say they want something, like Martha, but do nothing about it. The real question is: Are you *willing* to do what it takes to get what you want? I've done it myself – many times. For example, when it came to writing this book. I had been saying for three years before starting this book that I was going to write a book for women on investing. I'd say it, and do nothing. I'd say it again, and not write one word. I'd say it again, too busy. Finally a couple of very dear friends not so gently called me on it. "You're either going to get off your butt and write it or not!" was one friend's words of endearment. The other said, "Talk, talk, talk. So where is it?"

Carol

Another example of desire and no action is Carol. At one time Carol handled much of Robert's and my accounting and became my very good friend. We would meet twice a month to analyze our finances. We'd go over *all* the numbers. She'd see the different investments and rental properties we were acquiring and at each meeting she would ask me questions about investing. This went on for about two years.

Finally at one meeting she said, "I have a question about investing." I stopped her in mid-sentence and said, "No more questions! You've been asking me questions for years, and what action have you taken? What investments do you have?"

"None," she answered.

"So, no more questions," I declared. "I am not going to answer one more investing question; I'm not going to talk to you about investing – ever – until you go out there and do something. When you have your first investment then we'll talk again."

At our next meeting, two weeks later, Carol proudly walked in with a sheet of paper listing her first stock purchases. She said, "The stocks are just so we can start talking again. I really want to start buying rental properties. I promise I won't ask you any more real estate questions until I have my first property."

She kept her word. Within the month Carol found a small rental house, made an offer and had it accepted. Not having much money of her own she asked an investor who she knew well if he would become her partner on this investment. He said yes, and Carol was one her way. Since then she has bought a host of other investments including single-family homes and condos, as well as several apartment buildings. Today she is a very active investor… and we talk a lot.

Carol admitted to me later that in her mind she was taking action by asking so many questions. The light went on for her when she realized it had been two years and she had nothing to show for it. By asking questions again and again she convinced herself that she was "in the game." But it was really an excuse to not take action.

So the moral of the story is there is *talk* and there is *action*. And showing up is taking action.

What About Janice?

We had just started to move out of the kitchen and toward our study area when my home phone rang. It was Janice. I put her on speakerphone so we could all listen.

"I just wanted to let you guys know I was thinking of you!" she said loudly. "I know I should be there but I have great news!"

"What's the great news?" Leslie asked.

"You know how I've said again and again that I don't think I'm the type for a long-term relationship? Well, that may all be changing. I met this guy! His name is Greg. I haven't known him long. It's been a bit of a whirlwind. And, I can't believe I'm saying this, but I think I'm in love!" she blurted out.

Pat almost fell off the stool on which was sitting. "You? Miss My-way-or-the-highway? In love? I never thought I'd hear those words from your mouth. This could be exciting. Tell us all about him. How long have you known him?"

"Three weeks," she replied. "I know that's not long, but I think it's meant to be. We met at the coffee shop near my office. I ran in for a cappuccino, was waiting in line to order, and he walked in. We both kept looking at each other, and finally he came up to me, and we just started talking."

"What's his background? What type of work is he involved in?" Tracey asked curiously.

Janice rambled on. "We haven't talked much about that yet. I think he's been through some bad business experiences and he's not comfortable talking about them yet. I know he's worked for various companies, mostly in sales positions. At the moment he's in transition. He's figuring out what he wants to do next. He's very smart. He's got a lot of good business ideas. His mind always seems to be going a mile a minute. He's very excited about my business. He's even talked about working with me in my business. The more I think about it the more I like the idea. It does get tiring at times being the one doing it all. It would be great to have a partner to bounce ideas off of and to pick up some of the load.

"The reason I can't be with you this weekend is because we're flying up to San Francisco for a romantic weekend," she explained. "It was all his idea. He made the hotel reservations. He got us reservations at this wonderful intimate Italian restaurant that is almost impossible to get in to. It has like a three-month waiting list. He arranged everything."

Tracey couldn't help but ask, "You said he was in transition. What exactly does that mean?"

Janice explained, "All I know so far is that Greg had a setback from his last business venture. He started a consulting business, and about one year into it he ran into problems with his partner. He left the business two months ago and that's why he's searching for what he wants to do next. Having my own business I know how hard it can be at times, and after only one year apparently there was very little money coming into the business. It was just starting to take off. He'd be embarrassed if he knew I was telling you this but money is a little tight for him at the moment. We all have setbacks. And I don't mind helping him out financially for a little while."

Leslie naively asked, "So who's paying for your weekend in San

Francisco?"

"I am," she admitted. "Like I said, I don't mind doing that for a short time while he gets back on his feet. And he is really smart, which is why I'm thinking that the timing on this may be ideal. I ask myself, could Greg leaving his business and being available be the perfect opportunity for me to bring on a business partner? Everything seems to line up.

"And I know this is going to sound crazy," she said. "I know everything is happening so fast. But we're actually talking about Greg moving in with me! I've never even considered the possibility of living with someone. Tell me I'm crazy."

"You're crazy!" we yelled in unison through the phone.

"I know. I know. I'm excited and nervous all at the same time!" Janice said eagerly. "Gotta go! I'm off to the airport. Have a great couple of days together! Bye!"

I hung up the phone and the four of us just stared at one another in stunned silence.

Tracey spoke first. "Did I hear what I thought I heard? Did Janice say that this guy, whom she's known for all of three weeks, has no income? That she's paying for everything? That he might move into her home? And although it sounds like she knows very little about his business background, did she say that he's going to be part of her business? Tell me that's not what I heard?"

"That's what I heard," Leslie confirmed.

"What in the world is that girl thinking? Is she blind?" Tracey asked in total disbelief.

"They say love is blind. This may be the perfect example," I said.

"I guess time will tell," Pat said.

"He sounds like a freeloader to me," Tracey said.

We were all in a bit of disbelief.

"And on top of it, we were stood up for a guy!" Tracey was agitated. "I hate when women do that. How stupid is that?"

In a whisper Pat said, "Maybe he's just really good looking."

"Maybe he's good looking and young," Leslie added.

"Maybe he's good looking, young, and the heir to millions!" I added.

"Now that's finally beginning to make some sense," Tracey smirked.

We laughed as we envisioned the perfect man for Janice. But underneath the lightheartedness, we all had our concerns for her.

Chapter Eighteen

LET THE PROCESS BEGIN!

"You can learn new things at any time in your life if you're willing to be a beginner. If you actually learn to like being a beginner, the whole world opens up to you."

— *Barbara Sher*

The four of us walked out the back door toward the guesthouse that we converted into home offices. This is where we'd spend the next two days. We each took a seat at the heavy wooden conference table. A stack of legal pads and pens were in the middle.

"This feels quite official," Leslie commented. "Where do we start?"

1. Your Reason Why

"Let's start by talking about the reasons why each of you is here and why you have decided to do what it takes to get free, financially."

"Well, you heard mine when I walked in the door," Tracey started. "Maybe my company being sold is the best thing that could have happened for me because it definitely woke me up to the fact that, up until now, I was not in control of my life, on many fronts, but especially when it came to work and money. What really did it for me was when I realized that once the announcement was made I was actually waiting around for people who have never met me to decide what my future will be. I'm a name on a list that they can cross off at any time. So my reason why is that I never want to be in that position again. It's my life, and from now on I'll decide what my future is. And my first decision is to take control of my money. I now see how, by working for that paycheck every week, I've actually been controlled by money, and not in control of it."

Leslie went next. "I told Kim my reason why during one of our talks. Mine is very simple. I just want to paint. It makes my heart sing. I feel happy, confident, and full of life when I'm standing in front of my easel with a paintbrush in my hand. And because I spend so much time at my job I have less and less free time to do what I love. That's very simply my reason why."

We all turned to Pat next. I was curious to hear what Pat had to say because, to be honest, I was most surprised by her showing up that day.

Pat began quietly. "I've been doing a lot of soul searching since our very first lunch. It was at that lunch that I realized that for much of my life I was just going along with everyone else's dreams and goals, not my own. I was supporting my husband's and my kids' lives and totally put my own life on the back burner. After our lunch in New York I decided to move my life to the front burner and began asking myself what I truly wanted. And the answer surprised me.

"Our conversations about investing sparked an interest in me and, as you know, I love to research and dig up the facts, so that's what I did. I went online and began to learn about the investment world. It fascinated me. I went to Web sites and learned about stocks, stock options, real estate, investing in private businesses, precious metals, and so much more. I'd lose myself for hours in front of the computer taking in all this information. But I did all this in private. I didn't share it with anyone, including my husband. Then the hard part came. As I mentioned to you, my husband makes all the major financial decisions, and my concern was that if I brought this up to him he wouldn't take me seriously and that there'd be this big argument about the money.

She continued, "So I decided I would just tell him the truth. And I did. I told him how I felt I've been supporting everyone else and that I wanted to do something for me. For the first time, in a very long time, I wanted to put me first for a change. I told him I was hesitant to talk with him about our finances because money was always his domain. I explained what I had been learning online and that I wanted to pursue this not as a hobby but as a serious full-time endeavor. I said I've got a lot to learn, and I'd love his support on this. And then I held my breath and waited for his response."

"Did he go along with it?" I asked.

"I wish it were that simple," Pat answered. "No, he's not fully supporting me on this yet. But I'm determined that eventually he will. I believe in this enough to move forward without his blessing. He's one that will need to see the proof, and when he does I'm sure we'll be in this together. He feels so tied to his job now that that's all he can see. I wouldn't even say he's happy there, but that's what he knows. The longer he works at this job the less he seems to enjoy it. I want to show him another option and what I think is a much better option. So I'm actually doing this for me but also for him. I truly believe in the long run this will make our marriage stronger, which will be the greatest gift of all."

"Wow. Good for you," Leslie applauded. "Congratulations."

"Those all sound like three very strong reasons why, " Tracey acknowledged.

"They are," I agreed. "And they have to be strong because your reason why will get you through those times when things don't go as planned or when you start to doubt yourself or when others question what you're doing. It's always easy to quit. You all have compelling motives for wanting this. Well done!"

2. Where You Are Today?

"Before you can get to where you want to go, you have to know where you are," I said. "Could you imagine getting into a taxi with no destination in mind? You'll either go nowhere or spend the day driving around in circles."

"So what you need to do next is to find out where you are today, financially. What's your current financial status? And there's an easy way to figure this out," I assured them.

"I had this discussion with Janice when we last met. You first want to determine how wealthy you are," I said.

"OK, hold it right there. I'm already depressed," Leslie moaned. "Wealthy is not a word I would use to describe myself."

I laughed. "Here is the definition of wealth that I use: If you stopped working today, how many days could you survive financially? In other words how many days, months, years *wealthy* are you?"

We walked through the same process I went through with Janice to calculate each woman's *wealth*. (Chapter 11). Here are the steps they went through.

1) Pat, Tracey, and Leslie each made up their list of their monthly expenses.

2) Next, they added up how much money they have in savings, CDs, stocks that could be sold or liquidated today, and cash flow from their investments.

3) Next they computed: Income (Step 2) divided by Monthly Expenses (Step 1) = Your Wealth.

This is when the grumbling began.

"I'm not sure what this number means, but I don't think it's good," Leslie lamented.

"My number is 7.2," Tracey said. "What does that mean?"

"That means that you are 7.2 months wealthy. If you stopped working today, then you could survive financially for 7.2 months. After 7.2 months you'd have to generate more income."

"That's no more than an extended vacation!" she cried.

"I wouldn't complain if I were you," Leslie retorted. "My number is 0.6. That means I couldn't even make it for one month! I think I flunked this test."

I laughed. "There's no right or wrong answer here. Your answer is simply your answer. The purpose of this exercise is to simply know where you are today. That's it. And now you know."

Pat jumped in. "As best I can figure, since I'm not exactly sure of the dollar amount of our savings and investments – which in itself reveals how little I know about our finances – I'd estimate our wealth at about 10 months. Which is a bit of an 'aha' since I take it for granted that my husband will just keep working. But what if for some reason he couldn't work? Then that's not a lot of time before I'd have to come up with other sources of income for our family, like me working full-time. It would be next to impossible for me to support our lifestyle as a journalist who hasn't worked in 17 years!"

3) Your Plan – Where You Want To Go And How To Get There

"Now you all know where you are. Congratulations," I said. "Your next step is to determine where you want to go. And to do that, there are two questions to answer."

"What are they?" Pat asked.

First Question

"The first question is: are you investing for capital gains or for cash flow?" I started. "Remember when we discussed this earlier? When you invest, you're generally investing for either cash flow or capital gains. If you're a stock investor, then your primary focus is capital gains. You want the stock to appreciate so that you can sell it for more than you bought it. If you buy a house, fix it up, and immediately sell it, then you're investing for capital gains. Typically if you buy a house, hold on to it, and rent it out, then you're investing for cash flow. Stocks that pay you a dividend are cash flow investments.

"For me my two favorite words are cash flow. As long as that cash is flowing in without me working for it I am free. I just want to buy or create assets that at the end of every month generate a positive cash flow back to me. That's my formula."

Tracey made a good observation. "I know I don't want to work for the rest of my life. At least not doing what I'm doing now. And I can see that if I buy and hold onto investments that give me cash flow every month, and I keep doing that, then I will accumulate more and more cash flow. Eventually I can stop working, because

The first step is a realistic assessment of where you are.

The second step is to determine where you want to go.

as long as I own the investment the cash flow will keep coming in every month.

"On the other hand if all I buy are capital gain investments, then I must sell them in order to get any money from them. So I have to continually keep buying and selling in order to increase the income. On top of that it seems I'll end up with a finite amount of money to live off of. I'll have to accumulate a lot of money to support me until the day I die. They really are two different strategies."

"Exactly," I replied. "And please understand I'm not saying one strategy is better than the other. Cash flow is the formula I use. I started investing for cash flow in 1989. By 1994 Robert and I were financially free because of the cash flow from our investments. I'm not talking about amassing huge amounts of wealth. I'm talking about being free so that you can go on to do what it is you truly want to do.

"Let me say one more thing. My primary investment is real estate. Why? Because I love real estate. I love looking at properties. I love analyzing properties. I love searching for the upside of a property; how to make the best use of the property. And I love the cash flow. You have to find the investment vehicle that you love, otherwise you probably will not be successful in it.

"I have a girlfriend who I'd been encouraging to get into real estate for well over a year. She never got started. Then one day she attended a talk on how to trade stock options. She was hooked. Today she successfully trades stock options. She loves it, and because she loves it she's very good at it. So it's important to choose the investment that best suits you – the investment that you love."

Second Question

I recapped, "So that's the first question you need to answer: Is it cash flow or capital gains? The second question then is: What's your goal?"

"My goal is I want to be 100 percent free!" Leslie blurted out. "I'm crystal clear about that. I don't need a big mansion or fancy cars. I just want to paint. I hate worrying about money. I hate being told when to come in for work. I want to know that I am financially set for life and not have to work if I don't want to. I've already decided to pursue the cash flow investments. I want enough cash flow coming in to handle all my living expenses. And my living expenses come out to $5,200 per month. That means I need $5,200 per month in cash flow. That's my goal."

"That's very clear," Pat said. "I know this doesn't sound like me, but I didn't come here with a goal in mind. My thought was that I'd just start investing and keep building it up. But now, after going through the exercise and discovering that with my husband's salary and our savings, we have enough money to last just about one year. I need to rethink this. Who knows what the future holds? I'm certainly not prepared if something unexpected happens. Yes, I need to look at this a lot more seriously."

How To Get There

"Now that I have my goal, how do I get there?" Leslie asked impatiently.

"This is where your homework begins," I responded. "Now you create the plan that will get you to your goal. How do you want to get there? There are so many investment vehicles available to you that your job is to first, find the primary investment that you are excited to pursue. There's nothing worse than studying something in which you're not interested. That takes me back to my days in high school when I was forced to study subjects like trigonometry. I couldn't see how I would ever use it outside the classroom."

"I guess that's why I flunked biology," Tracey confessed. "Dissecting frogs was just not my thing."

Pat jumped in. "You're all going to laugh because this is so typically me. In my research over the past months I actually came up with a list of some of the different investments available. I e-mailed it to Kim, and she added a few more investments to the list. I brought copies for everyone."

Leslie said, "We're not laughing, Pat. This is great. Thanks!"

The following is Pat's list of investments. (More investments exist than are on this list but this gives you a good sample of what's available).

Types Of Investments:

Real Estate:	Single-family Houses
	Multiple-unit Properties
	(from duplexes to large apartment
	buildings)
	Office Buildings
	Shopping Centers/Retail
	Warehouses
	Self-storage Units
	Raw Land

Paper Assets:	Stocks
	Stock Options
	Bonds
	Mutual Funds
	Treasury Bills and Notes
	Hedge Funds
	Private Equity Funds

Businesses:	Privately-held Businesses.
	(You may be actively involved in the
	operations of the business or a
	passive/hands-off investor.)
	Franchises
	Network Marketing (You are building a
	business as well as building passive
	income through the distributors under
	you.)

Commodities:	Precious Metals
	Gasoline
	Oil
	Wheat

Sugar
Pork Bellies
Corn
Etc.

Foreign Exchange
Tax Lien Certificates
Inventions
Intellectual Property
Water and Air Rights

(Note: The definitions of these investments can be found in the glossary at the back of this book.)

"Pat pointed out the three primary types of investments: real estate, paper assets, and businesses," I explained. "And then, as you can guess from this partial list, there are a host of others. You can even invest in upcoming sports stars. Many athletes don't have the financial means to get to the big leagues, so an investor may provide the necessary funding for training, travel, and competitions. If the athlete makes it to the pros, then the investor gets a percentage of the athlete's winnings."

"It seems like you can invest in just about anything," Tracey commented. "So once you know the type of investment you want to go after. what exactly does a plan look like? How do you figure out 'how you want to get there,' as you say?"

"That's a good question, because often when people hear the words 'make a plan' they tend to make it far more complicated than it needs to be," I explained that 'How do you want to get there' means deciding on the following:

1. **What will my primary investment vehicle be?** You may invest in more than one type of investment, but I've learned that I'm most successful if I focus most of my time and energy on one type of investment.

2. **Within that investment category what type of product will I focus on?** For example, if you invest in stocks, what types of stocks are you going to focus on? What area are you going to become an expert in? For me, if I went into tech stocks I'd fail miserably because I have no interest in them and I know next to nothing about technology. If I chose to go into stocks I might put most of my attention into real estate stocks. If you choose real estate as your investment of choice, there are single-family homes, apartment buildings, office buildings, shopping malls, etc. Especially when you're just starting out, pick one thing that you can become an expert at and focus on that. Once you're comfortable with that investment, choose what you want to focus on next.

3. **What is my time frame for accomplishing my goal?** And what are my time frames for accomplishing the smaller goals along the way to my main goal?

"That's really all there is to 'how do you want to get there,'" I concluded. "You can make it more complicated if you want, but I caution you against creating some long, drawn-out, detailed plan that takes so long to put together that you never get started."

"What was your plan when you started?" Leslie asked.

I smiled. "Robert and I came up with our extensive and in-depth plan to become financially free. Our plan was this: to buy two rental properties per year for 10 years. That was our plan. We would focus on single-family homes. At the end of 10 years we determined that we would have a total of 20 rental units and the cash flow would be more than our living expenses. That was the entire plan."

"Did you make it?" Tracey asked.

"We did," I said. "But not in the time frame we originally

stated in our plan."

The three women looked a bit disappointed.

I continued. "Once I bought my first small two-bedroom, one-bath rental house, we bought a second and a third. In the process we discovered that it's just as easy to buy a multiple-unit building as it is to buy a single-family house. So instead of taking 10 years to acquire our 20 units, we had all 20 in just 18 months. Once we knew where we were and where we wanted to go and we stayed focused, the whole plan came to fruition much faster than I ever thought possible."

The rest of the day was spent studying, talking, writing, drawing, making phone calls, and researching online as each of the women put their investment plans together.

By the end of the day Leslie, Pat, and Tracey all had their goals in writing and a great start to their plans. They were each pleased with what they had accomplished. Leslie looked at the clock on the wall and laughed. "I can't believe it! It's almost 7:00! We were so into what we were doing we forgot to do our traditional girls lunch!"

"How about a girls' dinner?" Pat asked.

When creating your plan:

   1. Determine Your Goal

   2. Then Ask Yourself These Three Questions:

      – What will my primary investment vehicle be?
      – Within that investment category what type of product will I focus on?
      – What is my time frame for accomplishing my goal?

Chapter Nineteen

THREE TYPES OF MEN /
THREE TYPES OF INVESTMENTS

"I am extraordinarily patient, provided I get my own way in the end."
– Margaret Thatcher

Over dinner at a restaurant it became clear we had all put in a long day. The conversation surprisingly turned to men, and then it took a wacky twist.

I started the discussion. "My girlfriend Cherie and I were having this wonderful discussion about men. Just as men rate women on a scale of 1-to-10 as they pass by, Cherie and I were singling out specific men on the street and speculating what *type o*f man they were."

"You know," Cherie said, "There are really only three types of men in this world."

"Three?" I replied. "There are definitely more than three types."

"I'll give you the three types, and you tell me if there are more," she challenged.

"Deal," I said.

Cherie explained, "The three types of men in this world are the bad boys, the nice guys, and the wimps."

"I'm listening," I said.

"The bad boys are the ones your dad doesn't want you to date," she laughed. They're exciting, enticing – women can't resist them. They are the challenge. They are unpredictable, and you've always got to keep your eye on them. They are not boring. They will always hold your interest. You never forget them. And don't be surprised if they break your heart. If there is a love/hate relationship, chances are there is a bad boy involved.

"Next are the nice guys. We all know a few. They're your friends. Everyone likes to be around them. You can talk with them. They are comfortable to be around and they'll listen if you have a problem. You rarely get into fights with nice guys, because they'll talk it out before it gets out of control. They are safe and usually won't cause you a lot of headaches. They're predictable. You almost never get a kiss from a nice guy on a first date, because he's polite and respectful."

"And the wimps?" I asked.

"The wimps are the guys you just want to shake some life into," she declared. "They're dull! There's little excitement in their lives. A date with a wimp often ends early after a movie. Don't expect an impromptu evening of a rooftop candlelit dinner under the stars with a wimp. Wimps will not surprise you. They don't accomplish anything great, because they never want to rock the boat. They will never take a chance. They want everything nice and steady. Most everything is too risky to them. To sum it up, they just exist."

"Those are three clear descriptions," I acknowledged. "And you're saying that every guy on this planet falls into one of those three categories?"

"You tell me," she urged. "Think of one guy. Does he fall into one of the three categories?"

"Yes," I admitted.

"Which one?" she asked.

"Bad boy," I said.

"That figures," she laughed. "Now think of all the guys you can. I'll bet you that they are either a bad boy, nice guy, or wimp."

I ran through as many men as I could in about three minutes and sure enough I could identify each one as one of those three types.

"You win," I conceded. "There is no need for a fourth or fifth type. You've narrowed it down very well. My girlfriends will have a good time with this one."

The Bad Boys, The Nice Guys And The Wimps

Pat, Leslie, and Tracey were all laughing. I could see their minds spinning, categorizing the men in their lives.

"My boyfriend in college – he was definitely a bad boy!" Leslie exclaimed. "But what's funny is I married a nice guy. Maybe that's why we didn't last. Maybe what I really wanted was a bad boy."

Tracey grinned. "Bad boys send you flowers after the first date, and you get all excited. But if a wimp sends you flowers, you worry. Does he want more out of the relationship than you do?"

"The nice guys take you on the carriage rides but don't make a move on you. The bad boys are doing who-knows-what under the blanket!" Pat chuckled.

Leslie added, "When I didn't have a date for my high school prom I went with a wimp, because he was always available. He was such a sweet guy, but it seemed that all the popular girls were with the bad boys. And then I noticed when I was with a bad boy I became more popular."

"It seems to be so much about attitude," Pat said. "Think of The Fonz on the television show *Happy Days*. He wasn't tall, dark, and handsome, but he was definitely a bad boy."

"I wonder why women as so often attracted to the bad boys," I said.

"I have a girlfriend who keeps dating the nice guys, and it never lasts. But the one guy she never forgets is the bad boy she dated over five years ago."

"The bad boys are a bit dangerous. They have some mystery to them," Tracey said. "They take risks, so there's a chance for great potential. My husband is a nice guy. I knew when we married that our life together would be somewhat typical of the average two-income, house-in-the-suburbs type of life. And when I look back and think about my career and family, that's ultimately what I wanted – stability and a feeling of assurance."

Leslie commented, "For me, the lows are low with the bad boys, but the highs can be very high. There is a sense of the unknown, but the possibilities are countless."

"So who would you classify as the bad boys?" Pat asked us all.

I started, "Mick Jagger – bad boy."

"John McEnroe, Eminem, Charlie Sheen – all bad boys," Tracey added.

"And, of course, Rambo."

"What about the nice guys?" I asked.

"If The Fonz is a bad boy then Richie Cunningham from *Happy Days* is a nice guy," Leslie said. "He's definitely a nice guy. And how about Barney Rubble from The Flintstones?"

We laughed.

Pat smiled. "As for the wimps, Al Bundy on *Married With Children* is a perfect example. Homer Simpson is a good fit too."

Three Types Of Investments

We could have gone on all night listing every man on the planet. Instead the conversation went in another direction.

I said, "You know, just as there are three types of men, I bet you could classify investments by three types as well – the bad boys, the nice guys, and the wimps. As we could pigeonhole every guy we ever knew into these nice and neat categories, we could do the same with investments.

"I'm not sure I follow you," Leslie replied.

"If every investment was classified as either a bad boy, a nice guy, or a wimp, then what is a bad boy investment, a nice guy investment, and a wimp investment?" I questioned.

There are two types of investors – active investors and passive investors.

If you want to be financially free through your investments, then you have to be an active investor.

"I see what you're saying," Pat responded. "For example, the bad boy investment is more of a challenge."

"Exactly," I said. "The bad boys are challenging. You've got to pay attention to them and stay on your toes. Don't walk away from the bad boys, because they may not be there when you return. You have to be very involved with the bad boys. They can be unpredictable. The bad boys will be a bit more work, but they offer the greatest rewards… if you know how to handle them."

"And the nice guys will never hurt you… too much!" Tracey announced.

"Yes. The nice guys don't need as much attention as the bad boys, but you still can't just leave them alone forever. They need to be in communication with you to know that you care. They are much more forgiving than the bad boys. The rewards will never be as great as with the bad boys, but there isn't as much risk of them burning you either," I stated.

"And the wimps?" I asked.

Leslie stated, "The wimps are boring! They don't do anything!"

I laughed. "Perfect. You can ignore the wimps forever and not much will change. You don't have to pay attention to them. They actually don't expect you to pay attention to them; that's why they're wimps. There is almost no risk associated with the wimps, but then there is little-to-no reward either."

"This is great!" Leslie exclaimed. "Investments are just like men! Even better because an investment won't leave you for a younger investment."

"An investment won't talk back to you!" Tracey joked.

"And you'll never have to worry where your investment is at midnight!" Pat added to the fun.

We were laughing so much we didn't notice the number of restaurant patrons looking over at us.

Which Is Which?

Tracey got us back on track and asked, "So which investments are which? Which investments are the bad boys, which are the nice guys, and which ones are the wimps?"

I took out a piece of paper and wrote down the three categories:

Bad Boys   **Nice Guys**   **Wimps**

"Let's go through some of the different investments and see where they fall," I suggested. "What about stocks?"

"If I'm going to buy a stock and hold it for the long-term, then I'd say that's a nice guy," Pat responded. "Because I'll still watch it regularly to see what it's doing and pay some attention to what's happening with the company."

"But what if you're day-trading stocks?" I asked. "What if you're buying and selling stocks on a daily basis? You may only hold shares of a stock for a few hours before selling them. Often, day-traders sell everything they're holding before the end of the day."

Tracey answered, "I'd guess that's a bad boy, because you have to watch it throughout the day. You have to be very involved if you're day-trading."

"Good point," I acknowledged. "I'll write 'stocks – long-term buy' under nice guys and 'stocks – day-trading' under bad boys. What about stock options?"

Pat jumped in, "I've actually been researching stock options, because they've caught my interest. I believe there are two answers. If it's an option that expires in six months, meaning you have six months to determine if you made money on it or not, then it's a nice guy. You're checking it but not highly active in it. If, on the other hand, you're trading stock options on a daily basis then it's a bad boy, because you're watching the stock prices every minute. I have to admit those bad boys make me a little nervous."

"So, real estate can fall into different categories as well, depending on what type of real estate investment you have," Tracey reasoned.

"Correct. If I simply lend money to an investor friend of mine for the down payment to purchase a property, then in return create a note or IOU, which states the amount of interest she will pay me on the amount I loaned her, and every month my friend pays me interest on that note until the amount of the loan with interest is repaid, I would call that a nice guy. There's a bit of risk if the property isn't managed well and my friend can't make the payments, but if she's a wise investor and she knows what she's doing, then the risk and my amount of involvement is small."

"If she stops paying on your note, then your nice guy becomes a screaming bad boy!" Leslie laughed. "Now you've got a challenge, and it will demand your attention."

"What about a 50-unit apartment building that is run-down, has bad tenants and has 20 units vacant?" I asked.

"Bad boy!" they all yelled.

"Why?" I asked.

"If it's run down and has a lot of empty units, then that property will need a ton of attention and effort to bring it up to speed," Pat said. "Aha! Now I understand why my neighbor has such an up-and-down marriage. She's married to a bad boy!"

Leslie went on, "Once you've got the property operating smoothly, can it then go from being a bad boy to more of a nice guy. You still have to pay close attention to it but not nearly as much as before you fixed it up."

"Good point!" I said, impressed by Leslie's assessment.

"Mutual funds?" Pat offered.

Tracey grinned, "My personal experience says 'wimp.' I put my money in and hope that something good happens. Nothing has happened, except I've paid a lot in fees."

"I'd agree," I replied. "Same with a 401(k). You keep putting money in and very little happens over time."

Pat interrupted, "Except when the market crashed and so many of our friends lost huge percentages of their 401(k)s. The wimps then became down-and-out losers."

"I would say buying raw land is a nice guy," Tracey interjected. "You buy it and it just sits there. You don't need to pay much attention to it, although you do want to pay attention to any progress going on around it, such as other developments. And if you choose to build a retail or office complex on the land, then it takes the time, effort, and education and could easily transform into a bad boy."

"So what are some other wimps?" Pat asked.

"What would you say they are?" I countered.

"Does a savings account qualify as an investment?" she asked. "Because a savings account doesn't do anything. You put your money in and that's it. Plus the risk is zero but the reward, especially these days, is just about zero as well."

"Perfect example," I replied.

"CDs would be wimps. Just like my ex-brother-in-law – he sits around, earns little to nothing, and no one expects much from him," Leslie kidded.

"How about gold and silver?" Tracey offered.

"If I'm buying gold and silver, then I'd call it a nice guy," I responded. I'll keep my finger on the price fluctuations, but I know it will be there in the morning. Not like a bad boy."

Pat deduced, "The bad boy investments could really hurt you if you don't know what you're doing. And that's the reason we're here for these two days – to learn what to do so we don't get hurt."

"Great point. And you may still get hurt at times. There are no guarantees," I explained. "But as you continue to learn and know, the hurts you do experience won't be life-threatening."

"One more," Leslie said. "What about investing in a business?"

"Are you investing in someone else's business or is it your business that you are going to operate?" I probed.

"Let's say I was thinking of buying into an already existing business and becoming a partner in the business, so I would be operating it as well," Leslie clarified.

"I hadn't thought of it that way before," Tracey said. "I guess there are several ways you can invest in a business. In fact, my brother put a little money into a new business venture his friend had started. He has no active role in the company. He simply invested a small amount in anticipation of a making a return on his money. I'd consider that type of business investment a nice guy investment. Although I'd want to be sure that whoever is running the company knows what they're doing"

"If they have no experience and don't know what they're doing, then I'd call that investment gambling," I added.

"And if I were to start a business…" Leslie began.

"Bad boy," Tracey finished. "Talk about a lot of time, effort, and attention. That has to be close to the top of the bad boy list!"

Active vs. Passive Investors

"This brings up a really good point," I began. "There are two types of investors – active investors and passive investors. If you want to be financially free through your investments, then you have to be an active investor. I doubt you'll ever get there by only putting your money into passive investments. Mutual funds and 401(k)s are fine, but you'll need more than that if you want to be financially independent."

"How do you determine if an investment is active or passive?" Pat questioned.

I explained, "Any time you turn your money over to someone else to invest for you, and you have no interaction with or control over the investment, I'd call that passive investing. You're handing over your money and walking away. On the flip side, being an active investor is just that. You are actively involved in the investment."

"So, buying and managing a rental property would be an active investment," Tracey added.

"That's right," I agreed.

"It sounds like all the bad boy investments are definitely active investments," Leslie commented. "Which makes sense since all the bad boys I've known were very active."

"And a lot of the nice guy investments are also active investments, but the level of involvement is less," Tracey said.

"The wimps are 100 percent passive," Pat said.

"Like my ex-brother-in-law," Leslie said.

"A mutual fund would be a passive investment, as would a 401(k). I put my money in but do nothing else with it."

Tracey added, "And it seems to me that a lot of stock investors are actually passive investors. Most of the people I know who invest in stocks give their money to a stockbroker, and the broker recommends what to buy and sell. The investor is not actively involved. She may check the price of her stock, but she's not studying it or closely following what the company behind the stock is doing."

"I'd agree with that," I replied. "If you're simply buying a stock off a hot tip from the cashier at the check-out counter, then that would qualify as passive."

"Years ago we were sold life insurance, and the agent referred to it as an investment. That is definitely a passive investment, because all we do is keep paying for it. I have no idea what the specifics of our policy are," Tracey admitted.

Pat summed it up. "So if I buy an investment, stick it in the closet, and never pay attention to it until the day I sell it, then that would be defined as a passive investment. When my stockbroker calls my husband and says he recommends moving some of our money into ABC stock, of which we know nothing about, then that is being a passive investor. Or if I were to put money into someone's start-up business and forget about it, then, again, that is a passive investment."

"That sounds clear to me," Leslie said.

She added, "Real estate investing is a good example of an active investment. If I buy a house, fix it up, and rent it out, then I'm very active with that investment. If I own a retail strip mall and rent the spaces to store owners, then that is an active investment."

"But if you buy shares of a real estate investment trust (REIT), which is like a mutual fund for real estate, and ignore it until you sell the shares, then that is passive," I said.

Pat asked, "What if I'm buying and selling stocks, and I'm not day-trading but I am researching the companies and the industry, tracking their history and learning as much as I can about each stock that I do invest in, then would that be considered passive or active?"

Tracey jumped in, "I think it comes down to the word active. If you are actively involved, and in this case that would be researching and learning, then I would say you are being an active investor. Versus a person who is too lazy to learn and just wants someone else to do it for them."

"Well said," I responded. "I personally would not recommend

investing in anything you do not have knowledge about. Which is why you must be an active investor in order to have your money working as hard as possible for you."

"I'm much clearer now on my question about investing in a business," Leslie stated. "I can own and operate the business, which is very active. I can invest my money in someone else's business and be involved to some degree in the running of the company, which again is active, but less active. This could be anything from a physical working role inside or outside the company or keeping closely attuned to what's happening within the company and the industry. Third, I could invest money into a company and simply walk away. That would be passive."

"You answered your own question," I said.

To Sum It Up

"Here is what I understand," Tracey summarized. "There are three types of men, and there are three types of investments – bad boys, nice guys, and wimps. Each investment type fits into one of those categories. You can have very passive investments in which you have no involvement to highly active investments that demand your efforts and attention. And what struck me as most important is that it's not actually the investment that is active or passive, it's the investor!"

"Nice wrap up," I applauded. "To add to that, I'm not saying one type of investment is better or worse than another. In order to be a successful investor it's important to know the pros and cons of each investment type. Ask yourself, 'What are the risks and rewards of each investment I own?' Don't expect a mutual fund alone to cover all your financial needs in retirement. It's not designed to do that. Just as rental properties are not designed to be hands-off investments. Know which is which and choose the ones that fit your plan. And remember, if your goal is to be financially independent then you cannot be just an investor; you must be an active investor."

Chapter Twenty

THE FIRST FOUR KEYS TO BEING A SUCCESSFUL INVESTOR

"If you educate a man you educate a person; if you educate a woman you educate a family."
— Ruby Manikan

The next morning we were still joking about the three types of men as we walked into our meeting room.

As everyone sat at their places at the conference table I said, "Before you get back to creating your plans I want to share with you some of the investment keys I've learned over the years. Most I've learned the hard way, by making a lot of mistakes."

"If I can learn from your mistakes instead of making them myself then I'm all ears!" Leslie stated. "I'm sure some of those mistakes were costly."

"Yes they were," I replied. "But not only costly in terms of money, costly also in the way of missed opportunities and wasted time."

"Let's hear them." Pat said firmly.

Key #1

I began. "Key number one you are already familiar with. The first step in pursuing any investment is to:

Arm Yourself With Some Education

"It's all about education. The more you know the better you'll do. Do some homework before you begin investing. There are plenty of excellent resources available to you. A little knowledge beforehand can mean the difference between making money and losing money.

"You wouldn't jump into the deep end of a swimming pool without first learning how to at least tread water – you'd drown. Jumping into an investment you have zero knowledge of is no different – chances are you'll drown.

"One of the reasons we support the network marketing industry is because the really good companies educate their distributors. They educate them in everything from sales to finance to personal development. The good companies aren't looking just for salespeople they want to support people being successful in all areas of their lives.

"The Rich Dad Company is a financial education company. We do not sell or recommend investments. All we offer is education. It's then up to our clients to find the investments that suit them.

"We do have a product, along with the Rich Dad series of books, that I believe is a must for anyone who is serious about investing. The product is the CASHFLOW 101 board game.

"When Robert and I retired in 1994 people constantly asked us, 'How did you do it? How did you retire at age 37?' (Robert was 47.) One thing Robert and I have in common is that we love games.

"Most of us played games when we were young, albeit board games, hide 'n seek, tag, and, of course, 'make believe.' I remember at age 12 riding my bicycle down the street early on a Saturday morning feeling completely free and totally happy. I was on my way to play soccer. I grew up with sports, and to this day I love to play all sorts of games.

"In 1995 Robert came up with the idea to create a board game that shows the step-by-step process we went through to become financially free. Education has to be fun (just as making money and investing is fun). So we created the CASHFLOW 101 board game so people could have fun while learning investing. That board game is a real-life look at how Robert and I think and what we do as investors. What we are now finding, through all the testimonials we receive, is that about 85 percent to 90 percent of the people who write us telling us about their success in investing say that they play the CASHFLOW game regularly. The game gets people to take action.

"Here is a diagram of the Cone of Learning. This is a result of a study conducted by Dale in 1969. The study set out to show how individuals learn best. What is shocking is the bottom of the cone shows the least effective ways the people learn. What are they? Reading and lecture – the two primary ways our school systems teach *[I do, however, appreciate you reading this book]*. What are the most effective techniques for learning? Real-life experience and simulation. People learn best by doing. That is why we created a board game, a simulation, to teach the subject of investing.

Cone of Learning

After 2 weeks we tend to remember		Nature of Involvement
90% of what we say and do	Doing the Real Thing	Active
	Simulating the Real Experience	
	Doing a Dramatic Presentation	
70% of what we say	Giving a Talk	
	Participating in a Discussion	
50% of what we hear and see	Seeing it Done on Location	Passive
	Watching a Demonstration	
	Looking at an Exhibit Watching a Demonstration	
	Watching a Movie	
30% of what we see	Looking at Pictures	
20% of what we hear	Hearing Words	
10% of what we read	Reading	

Source: Cone of Learning adapted from (Dale, 1969)

"So I recommend that part of your investment education include playing the CASHFLOW game. You can buy it and play it with your friends or go to our Web site and locate a CASHFLOW Club in your area. CASHFLOW Clubs are educational clubs whose members get together and play CASHFLOW along with other investment educational activities."

"Let's play the game tonight!" Tracey insisted.

"That's a great way to end our two-day event," Leslie agreed.

"Along with the CASHFLOW game and the other Rich Dad products there are so many resources available. Books, CDs, DVDs, seminars, newspapers, newsletters, Web sites, and investment organizations. The list is virtually endless. You simply have to sort through the resources and seek out the information you want."

"Of course there is no better teacher than real-life experience, so don't think you have to spend years studying before making a move. Get a little education behind you then get into the game."

Key #2

"The second key, which takes a good deal of the fear out of investing, is this:

Start Small

"Whatever the investment you choose, start small, and expect to make mistakes. You will make mistakes. I say to women who tell me they fear investing because they are afraid that they'll make mistakes, 'You don't have to be afraid of making mistakes; you will make mistakes. I guarantee it. If you know that then you have nothing to fear.'

"I'll never forget the first mistake I made on my very first rental house. After owning the property for about six months the tenant moved out. I thought, 'Aha! Great opportunity. I'll raise the rent $25 per month!' Since I was only making a positive cash flow of $50 per month, that would increase my cash flow by 50 percent. I was patting myself on the back for figuring this out.

"The mistake I made is I didn't check what the comparable rents in the neighborhood were. If I had done my homework I would have discovered that the rent I was asking was actually at the top of the scale. As a result the house sat empty for three months so instead of making an extra $75 I lost over $1,500. It was a good lesson.

"So make your mistakes with small amounts of money. Learn the fundamentals. If you're buying stocks, don't bet the ranch on one stock. Buy a few shares. If it's real estate you're buying then start with one to four units, not a 150-unit apartment building. Don't expect to make a killing your first time out. This is a process whereby you learn as you go. Put your toe in the water, learn, and keep going. This isn't a lottery ticket.

To be an investor you've got to get in the game. I call investing a game because sometimes you win, and sometimes you lose.

The definition of an investor is a person, company, or organization that has money invested in something. If your money is not invested then you're not an investor.

"Years ago a friend recommended a book to me on the subject of tax lien certificates. Tax lien certificates are created when a property owner does not pay the property taxes on her piece of real estate. You pay the taxes on the property, and if she never pays the taxes you could end up with the property for only the cost of the taxes you paid. Or if she does pay, then the penalty the state assesses for her paying late is passed directly on to you along with the full amount of taxes you paid.

"I went out and purchased two copies of *The 16% Solution*; one for me and one for Robert. So first we armed ourselves with a little education. Then we went to the county seat, which is where you buy these certificates, and followed the step-by-step process outlined in the book. We purchased about $500 worth of tax lien certificates. With that small amount, we were in the game and learning the process first-hand.

"I've often found that people get caught up in choosing the best investment – the one that will pay out the best return. That can paralyze a person because who knows what the best investment is. You may look forever. By starting small you can get real-life experience on a number of investments and decide which performs best for you."

Key #3

"Just as Robert and I did with the tax lien certificates:
Put a Little Money Down

"There are three reasons why this is important to your success.

"The first reason is pretty obvious. Until you have some money on the line you're not in the game. Up to that point it's all theory. To be an investor you've got to get in the game. And I call it a game because sometimes you win, and sometimes you lose. The definition of an investor is a person, company, or organization that has money invested in something. If your money is not invested then you're not an investor.

"Which brings me to the second reason. A little money means a little risk. A lot of money could mean a lot of risk. Whenever I'm embarking on a new investment I take into account my lack of knowledge and experience with that new investment. I'm expecting to make mistakes, which may cost me money. I can learn just as much with a little money on the line versus a lot of money on the line.

"The third reason is the most valuable. Have you ever noticed how interested you get when your money is on the line? My neighbor recently purchased a new Lexus convertible. Before she considered buying it she had no interest whatsoever in cars. When she decided to buy a new car, all of a sudden she became the car expert of the neighborhood. She did so much research before making her final decision it was mind-boggling. But she did it because she now had a vested interest – her own personal money.

"Another example is my friend's son who is ten years old. One day he overheard his dad talking about buying silver. He asked his dad about silver and why he was buying it.

"I got a phone call one afternoon, and it was the dad. He said, 'My son, Ben, wants to talk to you.'

"Ben got on the phone, 'Kim, I bought 10 silver coins with my allowance! I paid $7.60 per coin, that's $76.00! Do you think I should keep them in my house or should I get a safe deposit box? I like carrying them around, but dad says I should put them in a safe place. I have 10 silver coins!'

"Ben watched the price of silver every single day. He told his teacher about it. She had Ben give a talk to his class about his investment. The price of silver that day was at $8.50 per ounce. He actually had the other students calculating how much money he had made since he first bought the silver coins! He is so interested now in silver, and he's learning about other precious metals. He's 10 years old!

"One side note: Ben does not excel at school. As shown with the Cone of Learning, he learns best by doing. Studies have found that only about 20 percent of students learn by the techniques the school system uses. Eighty percent of people are not geared to learn that way. Through his interest in silver, Ben is reading better because he goes online and reads about silver, and his math skills have improved dramatically because he is applying math to real life.

"The moral of the story is if you want to learn about a new investment, buy it… but just a little."

Key #4

"The saying goes, 'The grass is always greener on the other side of the fence.' People are always looking for that hot new market. Whether it's the newly discovered condo market of Las Vegas, the next tech stock mania, or the latest hip, chic business opportunity that 'everyone' is jumping into. The grass is always greener than the turf in your own backyard.

"Key #4 is:

Stay Close To Home

"No matter if you're just starting out or you are a seasoned investor I still recommend staying close to home. What does that mean? It means stay close to what you know. This is the exact opposite of acting on a hot tip.

"The tech stock bubble for most people was an example of people venturing far from home. Although the fundamentals had gone out the window, everyone and their sister was throwing money into tech stocks. People who had never invested in the stock market were betting that tech stocks would be their savior. As we all know the bubble burst, and people lost millions.

"Peter Lynch, former manager of the Fidelity Magellan Fund and author of *Learn To Earn*, said it best about stocks:

> "*Every time you shop in a store, eat a hamburger, or buy new sunglasses, you're getting valuable input. By browsing around, you can see what's selling and what isn't. By watching your friends, you know which computers they're buying, which brand of soda they're drinking, which movies they're watching, whether Reeboks are in or out. These are all important clues that can lead you to the right stocks.*

> "*You'd be surprised how many adults fail to follow up on such clues. Millions of people work in industries and never take advantage of their front-row seat. Doctors know which drug companies make the best drugs, but they don't always buy the drug stocks. Bankers know which banks are the strongest and have the lowest expenses and make the smartest loans, but they don't necessarily buy the bank stocks. Store managers and the people that run malls have access to the monthly sales figures, so they know for sure which retailers are selling the most merchandise. But how many mall managers have enriched themselves by investing in specialty retail stocks?*'

"These opportunities are not just close to home, they are right in front of people.

"On a trip to Singapore a woman approached me and said, 'I live in Singapore, but I hear the real estate market is very good in Orlando, Florida. Should I buy real estate there?'

"First of all I didn't know if Orlando was a good market or not. Second of all, it didn't matter if it was. She had never invested in real estate before. I asked her, 'Have you been to Orlando, or are you planning a trip there soon?'

"'Oh no,' she answered. 'I thought I would purchase the property over the Internet.'

"I typically don't give specific advice, but this was an emergency. I told her, 'Do not buy property over the Internet. If you're just starting out, do not buy property in cities you've never been to and are not familiar with. Look for properties closer to home. And, most importantly, get some real estate investment education.' I have no problem with people making mistakes, but there's no need to be stupid. This woman was setting herself up for one big costly failure."

Three Reasons To Stay Close To Home

"When it comes to real estate I like to stay close to home for several reasons.

"First, you want to keep your finger on the pulse of the area in which you're investing. You want to know if the rents are going up or coming down, are businesses or stores moving into the area, what are property values doing, is the overall trend of the area increasing or decreasing? These are just some of the factors you want to be on top of. So when a property does come up for sale, you'll be the expert on that area, and you'll know quickly whether it's a property you want to pursue.

"Second, if a problem arises on your property you don't want to have to catch a plane, rent a car, go fix the problem, drive back to the airport, and catch a plane home. That will cost you in time and money.

"The third reason why I recommend staying close to home is that if I think there are always better deals in other cities I'll spend all my time chasing down hundreds of potential properties all over the world. Instead, I focus on a few key areas, and it's amazing the number of good deals that appear."

My Biggest Investment Mistake

"Why am I so firm on this? Because the biggest investment mistake I have ever made… so far… happened because I didn't take my own advice.

"Robert and I were in Miami, and we came across what seemed to be an excellent investment. It was a single tenant commercial property leased to a major health club. It was an approximately 45,000-square-foot building. We agreed on a price, and we began ironing out the fine details.

"Because I had never purchased this type of property before and because I was not familiar with Florida, I brought in a real estate attorney to go through the agreement that was presented to me. The first problem was that my attorney was an Arizona attorney and did not understand the nuances of Florida law. The second problem was the seller's attorney, whose level of experience was suspect, did not like our attorney, and vice versa. So instead of this being a property negotiation it became a pissing match between the two attorneys, and my property was the fire hydrant. On top of all that, because this appeared to be a more complicated investment than I was used to, in a city I did not know, I allowed my attorney to negotiate on my behalf. Big mistake. I learned a real estate attorney's role is not to negotiate the deal. The attorney's role is to raise the questions and potential problems. It's then up to me to determine how I want to proceed.

"To make a long story short, this went on for five months. Much of this complicated by the fact that I had zero experience in the area in which I was investing. Understand, we were still working on the initial agreement. The inspection period hadn't begun yet.

"At one point I flew with Robert to Miami to meet with the seller face to face. Within minutes we had the last sticking points hammered out, and we flew home. The next day the agreement arrived on my desk and the seller's attorney had changed what we had agreed upon! And the seller was now on a flight overseas.

"Finally, after months of this, I got a phone call one night at about 10:00 p.m. from our broker, who said, 'The seller is taking the property off the market. It's gone.' I later discovered there were other problems. But at that point I had this sinking feeling in my stomach. All that time, effort, and legal bills – for nothing. I called the seller, and he verified that the deal was off.

"It was then close to midnight. I was stunned and angry. But I wasn't angry with the seller or the attorneys. I was furious with myself. The deal was complicated by the fact that I was in an area I knew nothing about, and I was not very familiar with that type of property. But deep down I knew there was only one cause for this whole mess. The cause was me – *I didn't trust myself.* I didn't think I knew enough. I was scared that I'd screw up. I let my fear get the better of me, to the point that it killed the deal. Looking back it was simply another real estate transaction with a few things to learn. It was a huge lesson for me.

"It was then about 1:00 a.m., and I was kicking myself harder. All I could think was: 'After all that time and effort, I've got to find a deal to replace this one!'

"I walked into my office at my home and there by my computer was a stack of real estate pro formas from brokers. (A pro forma is a flyer or brochure that gives you information about a property for sale, including projected income, expenses, and financing terms.) So I immediately started sifting through this tall stack that I'd neglected while I'd been consumed by this Miami property.

"It was 2:00 a.m., and I picked up the information on a property that was presented to me several months ago. The more I looked at it, the more I liked it. 'I wonder if there's any possibility that it's still available,' I thought.

"At 7:00 a.m. the next morning I called the broker, who I knew very well and trusted. 'Craig, you know that property we talked about months ago right across the street from your office? Is it still available?'

"'They actually never listed it,' he said. 'They were only presenting it to serious buyers. I'll call the broker and find out.'

"He called me back 30 minutes later. 'The broker said if you're interested they'd sell.'

"'What do they want for it?' I asked.

"'Full price, that's their offer,' Craig said.

"'What's it worth?' I asked.

"'Full price,' was his answer.

"'I'll take it.' I told him.

"The irony is that this property was almost identical to the Miami property. And because I knew the area very well, and I now knew a lot about this type of property, we had the entire deal closed in about 45 days. Plus in the process I met one of the best real estate attorneys of all time, who renewed my faith in attorneys.

"As it turns out, today this property is the best of all my investments in terms of cash flow, value, and location. So my biggest mistake turned into my greatest asset – both in terms of knowledge and in terms of cash flow.

"Do you want to hear the greatest irony of all? This property is two blocks from my home.

"As I said, I like to stay close to home."

Chapter Twenty-One

THE NEXT FIVE KEYS TO BEING A SUCCESSFUL INVESTOR

"Independence I have long considered the grand blessing of life, the basis of every virtue."

– Mary Wollstonecraft

"That's a tremendous lesson you uncovered – learning to trust yourself," Tracey said.

Pat pointed out, "I think that's a big issue for women, and especially when it comes to money and investing, because this is new for many of us. What was the greatest impact for you from that lesson?"

I answered, "I would say that most of my fear around investing disappeared that night. My investments simply became investments. Much of the emotion, the reaction, and the anxiety vanished. I learned that all of my hesitation and worry had nothing to do with the investment itself; it had much more to do with me. I guess I was finally able to separate me from the investment. Now when I consider an investment, I'm usually, though not all the time, able to analyze the investment for what it is, rather than let my emotions confuse the facts."

"These guidelines take a lot of the confusion out of the picture for me." Tracey said. "Are there any other gems that you've learned along the way?"

"There are five more points I think may be useful," I replied.

"Well keep going," Tracey urged.

Key #5

"The previous four keys lead up to this one:

Set Yourself Up To Win

"We all love success. We love to win. As Vince Lombardi, the football coach for the Green Bay Packers said, 'Show me a good loser, and I'll show you a loser.' We are in this game of investing to win.

"If you're just starting out it's especially important to experience some success from the beginning. By following keys one through four – getting some education, starting small, putting a little money down, and staying close to home – I believe your chances for success with any investment increase greatly.

"Make that first investment a win. Why is that so important? Here are three reasons:

"Number one: A little success early on builds your confidence as an investor. When you lose, especially on your first investments, then the doubts begin to creep in. Thoughts pop in your head such as, 'Maybe I'm not cut out for this,' or 'I don't want to lose more money,' or 'Who am I kidding, I can't do this!' It's a lot easier and much more fun to move to your second investment when you've had a win on your first.

"Too often I see people who decide to skip the small deals and move right to the big deal. Instead of buying the duplex they go for the 100-unit apartment building. They have no experience and do not know how to operate a large property so they make a lot of mistakes quickly. Tenants move out because they are not being responded to. Expenses are cut to the point where the curb appeal becomes unappealing, so fewer and fewer prospective tenants knock on their door. The vacancies increase. Before they know it, these people who wanted to skip the fundamentals are losing money every month until finally they say, 'See, I knew it. Investing in real estate doesn't work!'

"The investor who buys 200 stock options at $5.00 a piece and invests $1,000.00 may be a lot wiser than the first-time investor who buys 200 shares of the same actual stock at $30.00 a piece and invests $6,000.00.

"Self-confidence is a magnificent byproduct of investing success. It is also a crucial ingredient in achieving your financial independence. The more your confidence builds from those early wins, the more willing you'll be to trust your judgment when investing. And the more you trust yourself, the less fear will be a factor. Those first wins set the stage for your success beyond limits.

"Number two: There probably will be people around you who insist that investing is risky. They are the ones who can't wait to cut out the articles on the couple who lost their life savings in the stock market or the looming real estate collapse. They send those articles right to you. These people love to be right, and they live to say, 'I told you so!' I bet you know one or two people like that. They're waiting for your first investment to be a bust so they can get you on the phone and 'console' you with, 'There, there, sweetie, I told you investing was risky, but you had to find out for yourself.' You've made their day! So let's not make their life wonderful, make your own life wonderful. Prove them wrong! Success is the best revenge.

"Number three: You want to make money. That is the name of this game. I guarantee that as soon as you see that first bit of profit from your efforts everything becomes a lot more fun. Remember, it's a game because sometimes you win and sometimes you lose. But games are also meant to be fun, and making money is definitely fun!

A Risky Investor

"I mentioned risk in point number two. People often think that the investing is risky. That's not true. My investments involve minimal risk. People who think investing is risky are people who either do not invest or invest with very little education or knowledge about what they are investing in.

"For example, the woman in Singapore who wanted to buy property in Florida over the Internet – that's risky. It's more than risky; it's stupid. She had no knowledge of investment real estate, no knowledge of the Florida market, no experience with property management, plus she was thousands of miles away from her property. She was setting herself up to lose. If she had gone and purchased a property in Florida and lost money, she would have turned into one of those naysayers saying, 'I knew real estate investing was risky.'

"The truth is that the investment wasn't risky. She was risky. She had no education and no experience. She wanted to take short cuts. She wanted the quick and easy answer instead of putting in the time and effort to be a successful investor. As I said, she was risky, not the investment.

"Have you ever acted on a hot stock tip? People do it all the time. I've done it. Someone tells you that they've got the inside scoop on a stock that's going to go through the roof. 'It's going to the moon!' he says. 'You better get in quick.' And not knowing anything about the company or its products you jump in. That's risky.

"I have a friend who had what she thought was the greatest investment strategy in the world. Every morning, first thing, she'd turn on one of her favorite financial TV programs. Whatever stocks the talking heads were discussing at the beginning of the day she would buy. Her thinking was that if the TV newsperson promoted the stock then that would cause others to buy it as well and drive the price up. Before the day was out she'd sell. Initially she made money with her strategy. It was a bull market; the market in general was moving up. She didn't have to pay too close attention. But then the market turned down. She was certain that her plan would continue to work, and she stubbornly kept at it. 'I know I can make back the money I've lost,' she convinced herself. In the end she finally quit. She had lost close to $10,000. Her strategy was not based on any facts or fundamentals. Her strategy was based upon TV pitchmen and promoters – again, no education and no experience. That's risky.

"If you are going to put your money into an investment of any kind first learn about the investment, start small, put a little money down, and stay close to home. Set yourself up to win, especially on your first investments. Build your confidence. Of course you'll make mistakes, but the more mistakes you make, the more you will learn. The more you learn, the less your risk, and you increase your odds of success. So set yourself up to win from the start."

Key #6

"The next key is very applicable to women.

Choose Your Circle Wisely

"Your 'circle' is made up of the people around you. You probably have several circles in your life. You may have your family circle, your work or business circle, or your circle of girlfriends. If you have a hobby or play a sport, then you have a circle relating to those interests.

"And when it comes to investing you have an investing circle. These are the people around you who are involved with or support you with your investment goals. Let's talk about friends, mentors and women's groups.

"Number one: Choose your friends. My friend Jayne gave me some very thoughtful advice years ago. I was sharing with her a goal I had for our Rich Dad Company. It was a big and bold goal. I told her I wanted to tell people about this grand vision to make it more real in my mind. I figured the more people I shared my goal with the greater chance of having it come to be.

"Jayne's words to me were this, 'It's good to share you goal with other people, just be careful who exactly you share it with. Not everyone supports you getting what you want.'

"What? I couldn't believe it. I am the optimist. I tend to think the best of everyone and every situation. I usually give people the benefit of the doubt. And here she was telling me to be careful and guarded about who I tell my goal to.

"I soon came to understand from first-hand experience what she was saying, and I found out she was absolutely correct.

"I was at a New Year's Eve party talking with a group of four people about New Year's resolutions. A friend of all of ours joined us and very excitedly revealed her goal for the coming year. She said, 'I didn't tell anyone, but this year I had a health scare and ended up in the hospital for three days. It was because I have always put my health last on my list of priorities. So my new goal is to lose 30 pounds. I've already found a personal trainer to work out with three times per week.

I know I can do it!'

"The five of us applauded her goal and encouraged her to go for it. As soon as she walked away one of the women in the group turned to me and whispered, 'She'll never make it. She's tried this before, you know, and it didn't work. I don't think she's got the discipline.'

"And that's what Jayne meant when she said be careful who you tell your goals to. I don't know why that woman made such a negative remark about her 'friend.' Maybe it was because of jealousy, resentment, competition, or some sort of politics involved, but it was clear this woman was not 100 percent on my friend's side. And when you're striving toward a goal the last thing you need is other people's negative thoughts and comments interfering with you. Heaven knows our own brains conjure up enough of those irrational thoughts on their own. Who needs friends who add to the noise?

"Sometimes your success, or even just a new goal that would increase your success, may threaten someone or point out his or her lack of success. Someone who is not moving forward in life may be resentful of those who are or want to. So the way they make themselves feel better is to put down the person who is going for it. People do not like to be reminded of their own shortcomings.

"My friend Margaret, who has been in television for most of her working career made a good observation. She said, 'The reason soap operas do so well is that people love to see people with lives more screwed up than their own. Then they can say to themselves, 'See, my life's not so bad.' Seeing someone in worse shape then they are justifies their less-than-successful lives, and they can feel good about themselves again.'

"You can feel it when someone is genuinely happy for your success versus another who may say the word, 'Congratulations,' but you know they don't mean it.

"I admit I am very competitive; I love to win, and I have those twinges of jealousy at times. I feel it because someone else's success is reminding me of what I need to be doing in my life that I'm not doing. I think this is human nature. Now when I feel those twinges I make a conscious decision – instead of being resentful I do my best to use them to inspire and drive me to be better.

"So, the secret is to surround yourself with people who will sincerely support you and encourage you to reach your goals. I made a decision years ago only to do business and only to build friendships with people I truly enjoy being around. Life's too short.

> *"The truth is that the investment wasn't risky. The investor was risky. She had no education and no experience. She wanted to take short cuts. She wanted the quick and easy answer instead of putting in the time and effort to be a successful investor.*
>
> *The investor – not the investment – was risky.*

"So, as you venture into this arena of investing be a little cautious of whom you have around you. Share your goals with people who are like-minded and who ideally have similar goals – people who will pull you up, not pull you down. Seek out people who want to learn and grow and who will support you in achieving your wildest dreams. You may find yourself hanging out with new friends.

"Number two: Seek out mentors. Mentors are people who do what you want to do and are accomplished in their fields. You may have mentors for different areas of your life: investment mentors, business mentors, fitness mentors, personal life mentors. My good friend and investment partner, Ken, is one of my mentors. He owns one of the largest property management companies in the Southwest and he is an investor. He sees all sides of a property investment. What I love about working with Ken is that he and I will get together to discuss a potential property deal. We'll spend quite a bit of time analyzing the pros and cons of the property. Every time, after each meeting, I come away high as a kite because I leave knowing so much more than I did when I went into the meeting.

"The question many ask is, 'How do you find a mentor?' I don't have the magic formula for this. Most of the mentors in my life I seem to meet by happenstance. There is a saying: 'When the student is ready the teacher will appear.' I find that to be true. When you are committed and ready to learn, that key advisor may be right around the corner.

"Number three: Seek out a women's investment group. As I said earlier, I do believe women learn very well from other women. That is why I encourage women to form all-women investment study groups. To repeat myself, I support groups that are education-focused versus groups that pool their money and buy investments together. You want to choose your investment partners wisely.

"If you do form an investment group, set your standards high. Invite women into your group who are serious about their financial future and are willing to learn and to take action. Ask women into the group who are like-minded and open-minded and who are willing to explore new ideas and opportunities.

"Run the meetings professionally. Managing your money is a profession. Start on time. End on time. Have agendas for each meeting. I've attended a good number of women's groups, and the most successful and most effective ones are those that demand high standards of their members from the start.

"Investment clubs are also a good platform from which to invite in experts as guest speakers to enhance your knowledge. There are so many smart people in the world of investing, and I've found that the brightest and most successful are typically eager to share what they know. They may not have time to be a one-on-one mentor but they are usually willing to speak to an interested group for an hour.

"The main point is this: surround yourself with people (and this applies to all areas of your life) who will cheer you on, who will be honest with you, and who will encourage you to keep going, during the ups and the downs, to achieve your goals, specifically your financial goals."

Key #7

"Most people, when it comes to investing, want the 'hot tip.' 'Tell me what to do.' 'Just give me the answer.' 'I have $5,000, where should I put it?'

They want the quick fix. To be a successful investor it helps to remind yourself that:

Investing Is A Process

"Striving toward your financial independence is a process. It will not happen overnight. There is no such thing as a get-rich-quick scheme that lasts. It's like learning a new language; you don't become fluent in the language in one day. You first learn a few words and phrases and you keep expanding your vocabulary. You practice, practice, practice, and you learn how to hold a decent conversation. You probably make some embarrassing mistakes in the process. Eventually, if you keep at it, you are speaking the language fluently.

"Every mistake you make simply makes you smarter. I watched a video of R. Buckminster Fuller building a geodesic dome – one of his best-known inventions. A group of college students were erecting the dome he had attempted to build many times, but it never held; it always collapsed. This time the students were certain they had the correct specifications and that the dome would stand. As they were nearing completion and Fuller was watching from above, the dome collapsed one more time. The students were in disbelief, discouraged, and dejected. Fuller, on the other had, was ecstatic. He was jumping up and down with excitement. He said something like, 'I can see what we did wrong! This is wonderful. We are one step closer to building a successful dome!' Fuller wasn't upset that the dome didn't stand. He knew he was in the middle of a process, and each step of the process made him smarter and took him closer to reaching his goal.

"The process for me never ends. I'm learning every day. I know that mistakes are part of learning. Do I like making mistakes? No, it feels miserable at the time, but I know I have to make them in order to learn and to eventually get what I want. If I went for the multi-million dollar office building as my first investment in 1989 and it worked, then two things would have probably happened. First, I would think I was intelligent and actually knew something about investing when in fact I had gotten lucky. Second, I'd probably do it again, because I would think I was smart, and I would probably end up the big loser, because I would have no idea what caused my success in the first place, and therefore, I'd have no way to duplicate it. By going through the process and learning every step along the way you will be able to duplicate your success over and over again.

"Elizabeth Taylor, the actress, understood the process. She said, 'It's not the having, it's the getting.'"

Key #8

"In order to keep growing personally and to grow you investments there is no substitute for:

Always Keep Learning

"This is truly the key to success. Nothing stays static. The markets are always changing. The rules are always changing. To be a winning investor you've got to change as the market trends change. And that means you must always be learning. There are three positions to choose from; keep up with the changes, keep ahead of the changes, or get passed by by the changes.

"Karen, a very successful real estate investor told a friend of mine that she was attending a two-day real estate class offered by a private company. Karen asked her if she wanted to join her.

"'Why are you taking a real estate class? That's what you do every day. You're so successful. What can they teach you?' my friend asked.

"Karen responded, 'That may be why I do better than the average real estate investor. I'm always looking for that edge. There is so much new information. I never stop learning.'

"My friend didn't join Karen. My friend is a real estate investor as well. The problem is she hasn't bought or sold a property in more than three years because her old formula is no longer working, and she isn't willing to look for new answers. She decided to stop learning.

"And then there's my friend Frank, in his 80s. I think he'll live forever because he never stops learning. I get articles from Frank every week related to the world economy and investing. One week he's in

China reviewing the gold mine he took public. The next week he's in Vancouver, Canada, taking an art class. He invited Robert and me to a private opening in Scottsdale, Arizona of a new concept in condominiums. He often shows up at our Rich Dad seminars. He understands and uses the latest and greatest computer technology to make his businesses run more efficiently. He never stops learning. And I'm fortunate to keep learning from him.

"Continued learning takes effort. You're not going to learn how to run a half-marathon by simply researching it on the Internet. You've got to get out there and put the shoe on the pavement. It might mean finding a coach and starting with short distances and gradually building up to where you can run the 13 miles without collapsing from exhaustion. It not only takes physical stamina, but it takes mental stamina as well. You've got to keep exercising your mind.

"So, for your health and for your financial success, keep learning."

Key #9

"Now, I must insist that you never forget key number nine. It may be the most important of all. Promise to yourself that you will forever remind yourself of this essential personal rule. Promise?" I asked.

"Promise!" the women dutifully replied.

"Key number nine is this:

Have Fun!

"I highly recommend you celebrate each win along the way. Acknowledge yourself when you have successes. Your successes may be winning financially, overcoming an obstacle, putting your fear aside and going for it, realizing you haven't worried about money in months, or feeling completely confident and in control of your life. There will be many successes along the way. And those are fun and worth celebrating.

"What else is fun is seeking out that next investment, following the progress of each of your investment, figuring out how to increase the income and cash flow of your investments, learning something new that will make your next investment even better, and especially seeing the money come in. It's all fun."

The Wrap-Up

"Those are my nine primary keys for becoming a victorious investor," I ended. "Any questions?"

"Hundreds, I'm sure," Leslie said. "'Have fun' rings true with me."

"Remember you promised," I kidded.

"The picture keeps getting clearer for me," Tracey said. "I really understand now that this is a process. And as long as I'm investing, the process will never end. Because there is always more to learn."

"By the way," Pat offered, true to form. "I took notes on the nine keys. I'm happy to make copies!"

Chapter Twenty-Two

"Show Me the Plan!"

"Women are like tea bags; put them in hot water and they get stronger. "
– Eleanor Roosevelt

The four of us spent the rest of the day sharing ideas, defining more clearly what each of the women wanted, and then realistically looking at what it would take to get there.

By the end of the two days the energy in the room was high. We felt like we had just gone through a grueling workout, but it felt so good. We accomplished what we had set out to accomplish.

Each woman had her plan of action and as Leslie said, "I can't wait to get back home and put it to work."

Tracey, Pat, and Leslie were crystal clear that financial independence was what they wanted. Their specific plans on how to get there were different for each. To complete our two-day session each woman summarized her plan to the group.

Leslie's Plan

Leslie went first. "I knew before I arrived that my ultimate plan was to build up my cash flow so that I no longer need a job to support myself. As I told you all, I hate worrying about money and, even more, I hate being told when to show up for work and when I can take time for myself. What I'm going to do is to continue working, since that is my sole source of income at the moment, but I am going to take 20 percent, to start, of everything I make and put it toward an investing account. That will be a stretch for me, but I want to build up that account quickly."

Leslie continued, "I'm drawn to real estate. I can see myself owning rental properties, networking with people involved with investment real estate, and creating nice environments for people to live in. I already know of some neighborhoods near where I live that may be perfect for rentals. As soon as I get home I'll start researching those areas and, as you said, become the expert in just a few areas. I've even come up with two people I know quite well who may actually have a sincere interest in partnering with me. I'll approach that cautiously. They are both self-made so I know I'll learn something just by talking with them. I know I've got my work cut out for me, but I am so ready."

Tracey's Plan

Tracey took a bit of a different approach. "The sale of the company I work for has really opened my eyes. I never realized what little control I had over my own life as well as how dependent I was on my job. I love the business world, and I would love to work for myself. The timing is perfect. Even if my company does keep me on, I'll never get ahead because the reason I've done so well there is that I've committed my life to that company and my job. I'm in my office by 6:30 a.m., and I rarely get home before 8:00 p.m. And then when I'm not at work I'm thinking about work. So I need a drastic change."

"Here's my plan," she explained. "I'm going to sit down with my husband and closely review our current financial needs. Then I want to do two things. First, I am going to begin working for myself. I could pick up three projects tomorrow if I wanted! Several people I know outside of my company have been asking me to work with them on a project management basis, so now is as good a time as ever. There are three projects I could take on tomorrow. That won't take up all my time, although I'm not kidding myself that it will be a walk in the park. I'll probably make as much as, if not more than, what I'm making now with just those three projects alone. Second, I'll make the time to build up our investments. I'm with Leslie; I only want to acquire assets that throw off cash flow. I'm not certain which specific investments I want to pursue. I'm leaning toward real estate and businesses that I don't operate. I see my husband and me doing this together. I know he'll be very excited when I present all of this to him. So the second step is to determine which cash flow investments we both want to pursue. I promise I'll have that answer to the three of you within one week. I don't want to lose any momentum from these two days. You know, what excites me the most is that for the first time since I can remember I finally feel like I am back in control of my life."

Pat's Plan

"I seem to have a natural interest in stock options," Pat said. "Maybe because of my knack for researching, I'm very comfortable online and the world of trading options fascinates me. I have to confess that a lot of the research I've done over the past few months involves options trading.

"So here is my plan," She said. "I am going to immerse myself into learning how to trade stock options. And from what I understand this is not a simple subject, so I want to learn from the best. I'll locate the top programs and instructors on the subject. And I will start very small and only put a little money down. I get so energized just thinking about it!"

She went on. "I never gave up my writing completely. I have a nest egg of my own from various assignments that have come my way over the years. I'll use some of that money to fund my education. I realize that the money I make from trading is considered capital gains and cash flow investments are ultimately the way I want to go. Therefore, any money I make from my stock option trading will go into my cash flow investing account. That money will eventually go toward purchasing investments that throw off cash flow.

"So, I'll make my money through trading stock options. The money I make will then buy my cash flow investments. This plan works for me because it allows me to make my own money through

I've learned to trust myself. And the more deals I do, the sharper my intuition becomes.

The biggest mistakes I've made, not just in investing but in life, are the times when I didn't trust myself – when I allowed people to persuade me to take actions that I didn't agree with but I went along with anyway.

investing without depending on my husband. If he decides to join me, great, then we can work this plan faster. And this would be my ideal. But if he doesn't, I'm still on my way to becoming financially independent.

"Two more things," Pat added. "I've already made phone calls back home to two women who say they want to start an investment study group. I'll see how serious they are when I meet face-to-face with them. I think the ongoing support would be so helpful. And then I had a really fun, off-the-wall thought. Royalties from books are a good source of passive income. This is something that, as a writer, I always wanted to do – write a novel. I actually have the start of a book that has been sitting in my computer for years. Now I know this is a long shot, but I never considered a book as a source of cash flow or passive income. As a writer I just dreamed of getting a book published. But now I see that it's possible to include my love of writing into my financial plan. I also plan to write more articles to submit to newspapers and magazines for sales as a source of income toward my investments. The main thing for me, as Tracey mentioned, is to keep the momentum going that I've gotten from these past two days. I am so excited."

To Do vs. To Have

Leslie added to that. "That's a good point," she said. "There is a lot to do and I don't want to lose focus once I leave here. I know that's why it's important I have someone or some people around me who are on the same path as I am. But how do I not let all the 'to do's' become so overwhelming?"

"That's a good question," I replied. "If you focus on all that you have to do, it can definitely deflate your enthusiasm, because it can overwhelm you. I asked the same question years ago and someone I greatly admire explained it this way.

"You may be familiar with the concept of

BE – DO – HAVE

"BE is your beingness; who you are. DO is the doingness; what you do. HAVE is your havingness; what you have. So who you are and what you do determines what you have. For example, if you want to have a baby then who you have to be is a mother-to-be and what you have to do is get pregnant, get doctor check-ups, take care of your health, prepare for the baby, and finally give birth. The key is that your focus from the start is not on all the things you have to do, your focus is on what you want to have – 'I want to have a baby.'"

I continued. "All you have to focus on is what you want to have because what you want to have is a much stronger motivator than what you have to do. Pat, if you want to have an article published in Time magazine then who do you have to be?" I asked.

"I have to be a first-rate writer," she answered.

"And what do you have to do?" I asked.

"I have to find out what type of articles *Time* magazine wants. I, personally, may have to take some writing courses to brush up on my skills, I have to research the article and then write the article. I must find out whom to submit the article to, submit it, and follow up. If my article gets rejected, then I may keep repeating the process until my article gets published. It's difficult to know all the steps along the way. Actually, if I did know all the steps in the process I'd probably never get started," she responded.

"That's the point," I said. "Concentrate on what you want to have and what you have to do will happen. Up to this point who you are and what you do have gotten you what you have today. If you want to change what you have, which is what we've been talking about for these past two days, then you have to change who you are and what you do. If you don't then you'll remain with what you have, and from what I've heard from each of you, you want to change and improve what you have. Correct?"

They each nodded.

"How do you change who you are?" Tracey asked.

I said, "Take Pat's example. If she wants to sell her article, then she has to become a first-rate writer. And no offense to Pat, but today she is not a world-class writer because she's out of practice. So she has to change who she is. As she said, she may have to take writing classes to improve her writing, get up-to-date with the publications she is writing articles for, possibly meet the key editors and form relationships with them, take rejection when her articles are turned down, and rewrite and re-submit. By doing all of that she will change who she is. She will go from being a mediocre writer to being a great writer. Does that make sense?"

"It does," Tracey replied. "So, for me to achieve my goals I have to be a successful business owner, which I am not today, as well as an excellent investor, which I'm also not. So it's my goal or what I want to have that determines who I become and what I do."

"Exactly. And most people first look at all that they have to do, which seems like too much work, and they never get what they want to have," I added.

Pat thought out loud, "It's like when someone says, 'If I knew what it was going to take, I'd have never started!'"

"That's so true," Leslie said. "I'll just concentrate on what I want to have, which is my first rental property, and who I become in that process and what I have to do to get there will take shape."

Trust Yourself

"I know it's getting late, but I have one last question," Tracey put forward. "I know at work when I have a tough decision to make, once I've got the facts the determining factor often lies in me and in my gut intuition. Does this play a part in investing? Because I would think 'women's intuition' could be a plus."

"I can only give you my experience with this. The day before I was to close on my first rental property, I was still wavering back and forth. 'Yes, I should buy it.' 'No, I shouldn't buy it.' I was driving myself crazy. In the end I said this to myself, 'You've gathered as much information as you can. At this point you've got to trust yourself.' I asked myself, 'Is it a go or a no-go.' The answer came back, 'It's a go.' The next day I bought the property, and it turned out to be a terrific investment."

"Now if I started with the 'go, no-go' question without doing my research and getting the facts, and I based my entire decision on my gut feeling alone, then that would have been foolish. I've also found that the more deals I do, the sharper my intuition becomes. I sometime ask questions and wonder, 'Why did I ask that question?' and it turns out to be the key issue of the entire deal."

"Early on in my investing life I purchased shares of Coca Cola through a stock broker whom I met through mutual friends. I bought it and didn't pay much attention to it until one day when I checked the price and noticed that I had made a nice profit on the stock. I called the broker and said, 'I want to sell my shares of Coca Cola.'

"He came back quickly with, 'No, don't sell now. I'm certain it's going to continue up. Look, I'm a professional, I know what I'm talking about it.'

"I told him, 'It may very well go up, but I'm happy with the profit, and I want to sell.'

"He continued on about how much more money I would make and how upset I'd be with myself if I sold today. Eventually he talked me out of it, and I didn't sell. Within one week the stock began to fall. In the end I sold my stock for a loss. That was a case of not trusting myself and my intuition.

"I have to say that the biggest mistakes I've made, not just in investing but in life, are the times when I didn't trust myself – when I allowed people to persuade me to take actions that I didn't agree with but I went along with anyway. It's the times when I am not true to myself, when I go against what is congruent with my thoughts and beliefs, that get me in the most trouble.

"I agree with you, Tracey. I think intuition plays a key role in the world of investing. I constantly listen to it. I just don't build my entire case around it; I don't lead with it. But I am always checking in with my gut feeling. I do my homework. I gather my facts. And I check in with myself. If everything lines up, then I move forward."

"My intuition tells me that we are all going to do really well with this," Leslie laughed.

"Let's take a quick break, and then I have one last story before we wrap it up," I announced.

Chapter Twenty-Three

FULL THROTTLE!

"A ship in port is safe, but that's not what ships are built for."
– Grace Hopper

"I want to share one last story with you, and then it is time to celebrate," I declared.

A Special Gift

"On Christmas Day 2004 Robert handed me a gift to open. He was especially excited about this particular gift. His eyes were fixated in anticipation on the present. I couldn't unwrap it fast enough for him. I tore the paper off of the small box, opened it and, viola! There it was:

4-day Grand Prix Driving Course
The Bondurant School of High Performance Driving
Phoenix, Arizona.

"I looked at him a little puzzled. This item was nowhere to be found on my Christmas list.

"'I bought one for you and me!' he exclaimed.

"'Oh, now it made sense,' I thought. 'He bought himself a gift and wrapped it up for me to open.'

"'Why a racing school?' I asked.

"'I thought it would be fun,' he said. 'And we like to learn together, so we can do the program together!'

"A car racing school was never high on my list of things I want to accomplish before I die. But we signed up and set the date."

The First Day Of Race School

"We were on the freeway driving from our home to the Bondurant School, which sits out in the desert, for our first day of class. I had no idea what to expect. I have to admit we were both a little nervous and apprehensive. I had never been on a race track in my life. When we arrived we registered and took a seat in the classroom – so far, so good. The instructors walked in, welcomed us, and made a few opening remarks. One instructor recommended we sign up for insurance because he said, 'If you damage the car, then you have to pay for it.'

"'Damage the car?' I thought. 'I might crash my car?' 'This is just great.' I was no longer nervous. Nervousness had turned to terror.

"Each student in the course was asked to stand up and say why they were there. There were twelve of us in the class. As the introductions were made, Robert and I looked at one another with expressions of 'I think we've made a big mistake.' It turns out the other ten people in the class were either professional or amateur race-car drivers. They were there to brush up on their skills. Robert and I were the only people from Arizona. The rest of the drivers were from Europe, South America, Japan, and all over the U.S. When my turn came I stood up and announced, with my voice shaking, 'I'm here to have fun.' And quickly took my seat. I felt I was in so over my head I just wanted to bolt out of there. Oh, on top of it, I was the only woman in our class.

"The instructors continued to talk and explained what we were going to do in the first hour. 'You will be assigned to your own Corvette. We are going to run you through various obstacle courses and speed tests. In your last test you will drive your car at full speed down the straightaway, and when we signal you, your job is to slam on the brakes as hard as you can and come to a complete stop within seconds.'

"Yes, terror was alive and well in me.

"We each select and get into our one-piece red racing suits and helmets. With each step toward my car, my heart was pounding louder. I kept thinking to myself, 'What in the world have I gotten myself into?'

"I warily got myself situated behind the wheel of my Corvette – #04. I moved the seat into position, adjusted the mirrors, figured out how to get into my seat belt, and then took a deep breath, turned the key, and started the engine.

"My instructor, Les, leaned his head in my window and said, 'Everyone will follow the lead car, one car behind the other, onto the racecourse. Have fun!'

"'Why did I ever say I was here to have fun?' I asked myself. That was a mistake. I put my foot on the gas pedal and realized there was no turning back.

"I have to commend the Bondurant Racing School for their teaching ability. There I was, someone with absolutely zero car racing experience, and through their instruction, I completed exercise after exercise, breathing heavy all along the way. At times my instructor would get in the driver seat or passenger seat of my car to better demonstrate what he wanted me to do. So I always felt that I had a safety net if I needed it. It's a program I highly recommend. The Bondurant School definitely took me beyond where I thought I could ever go. Just be prepared for this – there were only two emotions I experienced for the entire four days; sheer terror or utter exhilaration. There was nothing in between."

Racing Day Two

"Each day I experienced a new level of fear. On day two we were briefed on the agenda for that day. I think the briefing was more terrifying that the actual driving. Hearing about what we were going to do sounded unthinkable to me as I sat in the classroom. On day two we would be on the actual racetrack… and we would be racing against one another. I glanced at Robert across the room and silently said, 'This was your crazy idea. What are we doing here? Just remember…

"Are you going full throttle?" the driving instructor asked me. "Kim," he said, "you didn't come this far to come up short now."

'Going full throttle' became my new metaphor for life.

this is all your fault!'

"I did it all. My biggest win that day was when we were practicing race starts. We were instructed to position our cars on the racetrack bunched closely together. We drove, as a pack, at slow speed to simulate an actual start of a grand prix race.

"So there we were, cars grouped together, driving slowly around the track, no one could pass another until the flag was waved. I was looking toward the tower where the instructor stood with the flag, waiting for the signal. All of a sudden the instructor waved his flag and we were off! Every driver jockeyed for position, each wanting to take the lead. We did this a number of times. The first couple of times I backed off and let the other drivers pass me. Fear overtook me. On the third start I knew I needed to be more aggressive. We lined our cars up. I was more toward the front of the pack this time. We drove in second gear around the track waiting for that flag. I watched intensely, and there it was – the instructor waved the flag, and I took off. I got away from the group around me, and there was just one guy in front of me who was late on the flag signal. I blew past him and took the lead! 'Not bad for a woman,' I said sarcastically to myself. I later found out that the guy I overtook was so upset to be beaten, especially by a woman, that it made my victory even sweeter for me."

Racing Day Three

"Day three was as frightening and as exhilarating as the previous two days. Just when I relaxed and felt a moment of calm, the instructors would raise the bar one more time. The gradient built with every exercise they took us through.

"At the end of day three we were back in the classroom for the end-of-the-day debrief. That's when they announced the agenda for day four. My instructor began, 'These past three days you've been learning the fundamentals. You've been taught how to handle your car in slides, spins, turns, etc. Tomorrow you put it all together. Tomorrow you turn in your Corvettes. You will be assigned a Formula 1 racing car, and you will be racing at full speed against one another on the racetrack. And since a Formula 1 car seats only one person, your instructor can only instruct you when you pull into the pit. They cannot be with you in the car. You are on your own.'

"For those of you who are not familiar with racing, as I wasn't, a Formula 1 car is truly a race car. The cockpit of the car, where you sit, is so small you literally have to slither into the seat with your legs straight out in front of you, feet on the pedals.

"My adrenaline was pumping. Hearing my instructor talk took me to a whole new level of fear. Robert and I didn't say much to each other that evening as we drove home. My head was reeling, thinking about what I was about to undertake the next day. My mind kept replaying those fiery race car crashes you see on ESPN. How would I ever get to sleep?"

Racing Day Four

"This was the moment of truth. As I walked into the classroom it was more quiet than usual. The only ones having conversations were the most experienced professional drivers. The rest of us were silently pretending we weren't scared to death.

"The instructor walked into the room and began explaining what to expect that day. He really got my attention when I heard, 'If your car spins out of control, if you run off the course, if you damage your car or run into another driver…' The rest was a bit of a blur after that.

"I walked into the women's locker room to suit up. Since I was the only woman in the course I always had the locker room to myself. This gave me even more time to quietly build up the terror inside of me. 'I can't believe I paid to do this,' I thought. 'This is the craziest thing I've ever done. I should have known the first day when they sold me insurance. I could always pretend that I'm sick. What do you mean, pretend? I am sick!' All these thoughts raced through my mind.

"I stepped outside, and Robert was waiting for me. We walked silently, and somberly hand-in-hand across the parking lot toward the warehouse where the Formula 1 cars were stored. It felt like day one all over again. The instructors took their time making sure everyone was properly fitted to their car. I was led to the car that I would drive that day. My instructor, Les, smiled at me and made a few jokes to get my mind off the fear. The cockpit was so confining that sliding into the driver's seat was like pulling on a pair of jeans that were two sizes too tight."

Start Your Engines!

"Once in the car with seat belts fastened and mirrors adjusted I practiced my gear shifting, which was quite different from the Corvettes we had been driving. The large doors to the warehouse opened, and the next words I heard were, 'OK, everyone, start your engines.' I took a deep breath and after my third nervous attempt my engine started. Then one at a time, in single file, we slowly followed the lead car out of the warehouse and into the pit of the racetrack. With my helmet on I could hear my every breath. I was completely focused on getting my car to the track, nothing else. In the pit, my instructor gave me some final instructions and said, 'When you're ready, go onto the track and take some slow laps to get the feel of the car.'

"I sucked in every bit of courage I had and very slowly drove out of the pit and eased onto the track. By this time most of the more advanced drivers were already on the course and moving at a good speed. As I came up on the first curve I was yelling instructions out loud to myself of what to do. 'Down shift! Down shift! Apex! Apex! Apex! Hit it! Go! Go! Go!' I made it through the first turn. My adrenaline was soaring. I picked up speed. With each lap I felt more confident. Then the instructors signaled us all in, and we ran through a couple of exercises with them leading us on the track.

"After about two hours of getting comfortable in our cars they were convinced we were ready to race. 'When you see the checkered flag, that means it's time to come off the track. Take one cool-down lap and come into the pit.' One of the instructors reminded us, 'Let the faster cars pass. If you get in trouble on the track just raise your hand and someone will come to help. The last three days all come together now.

Good luck!'

"With that we all put on our helmets, worked ourselves into our cars, and headed out on the track. I was feeling pretty good about getting this far. I was on about my tenth lap when I approached the turn just before the straightaway. As I went into the turn I missed my downshift and my car came around the curve too fast. As I struggled to keep control of my car it began to go into a spin. Without even thinking I automatically responded and did exactly what I was taught two days earlier, and after about four or five complete spins my car came to a stop in the middle of the track, facing backward. 'Wow! I did it!' I thought. 'I just handled one of my top fears of racing – losing control of the car. I lost control, and I'm OK.' I was thrilled with myself. My confidence was growing by the second."

A Life-Changing Lesson

"I turned my car around and took off on more laps. But then I noticed that even though I was actually racing on the track, taking laps, keeping my car in control, I was getting frustrated. When I drove the Corvette, drivers passed me but I also passed a lot of drivers. I kept up with everyone else. In the Formula 1 car everyone was passing me. I wasn't passing anyone. I couldn't figure out why. I struggled with this through a few more laps, then I finally pulled my car into the pit.

"Les came up to me. 'You're having a hard time out there, aren't you?' he asked.

"'Yeah. I don't understand it,' I responded. 'I had no problem passing cars in the Corvette, but today everyone is passing me. I feel like I'm going so slow.'

"And then he said the words that truly changed my life. Les said, 'Tell me this, are you going full throttle?'

"'Full throttle? You mean is my gas pedal all the way to the floor?' I asked.

"'Yes. That's what I mean,' he answered. 'Are you full throttle?'

"I quickly said, 'No. I'm not.'

"Les pointed toward the track and said, 'They are.'

"'And that's why they're passing me, because they're going full throttle?' I said. 'I don't know if I can do that.'

"And then Les looked me in the eye, smiled, and said the magic words, 'Kim, you didn't come this far to come up short now.' And with that he walked away.

"'Damn!' I thought. 'It never ends. Even in the last few hours of the course I'm still being pushed to go further.'

"I sat in the pit for a few minutes. I knew Les was watching me. Slowly, I drove to the entrance to the track, not sure what I was going *to* do. I waited for an opening, sped up, and I was back on the track. I took a lap and kept hearing Les' words, 'You didn't come this far to come up short now.' And into the second lap I put the pedal to the metal, as they say, and in seconds I was going full throttle. Before I completed the lap I passed my first car, and I was screaming ecstatically at the top of my lungs. I was back in the race.

"What amazed me is that I found it was actually easier to drive and to take the turns when I was driving at full throttle than when I was holding back. It was exhilarating! I was so focused on my driving, maneuvering every single turn, that I never saw the checkered flag. As I came onto the straightaway there were the three instructors standing in the middle of the track, all waving checkered flags. I was the only person left on the course. Everyone else had been in the pit for a while. I laughed to myself as I took my cool-down lap and came into the pit.

"I stopped my car and I was beaming as I took off my helmet. Les was right there. 'You did it! Congratulations!' he said.

"'It was the best! I felt I actually drove better going full throttle. This is my new metaphor for life!' I exclaimed.

"'There is something I didn't tell you,' he said. 'I didn't want to give you a justification or an excuse for not going for it. '

"'What are you talking about?' I asked.

"'Most women who go through this course, at first do not go full throttle in the Formula 1 cars,' Les started.

"'Just like me,' I said.

"'Yes, except there is one difference,' he continued.

"'What's the difference?' I asked.

"Les said, 'When they come into the pit and I have the same discussion with them as I did with you – 90 percent of the women still do not go full throttle. They come up short. They don't go for it. I didn't tell you that because I didn't want you to say to yourself, 'Most women don't go for it, so I don't have to go for it either.' The key is this: if you don't go full throttle, then you miss what this sport is all about.'

"I silently thought to myself, 'And if you don't go full throttle, then you miss what life is all about.'

"That course changed my life."

Chapter Twenty-Four

DINNER WITH THE GIRLS – A CELEBRATION

"From birth to age 18, a girl needs good parents. From 18 to 35, she needs good looks. From 35 to 55 she needs a good personality. And from 55 on, she needs good cash."
– Sophie Tucker

"I think you just raised the bar," Tracey commented.

I just smiled.

"OK, let's call it a day… or two," I announced.

We were all ready for a nice leisurely dinner.

We got changed, jumped in my car, and drove, not at full throttle, a short distance to a wonderful Italian restaurant known for its homemade pasta and fresh calamari. The valet parked the car, and the host greeted us as we walked in. "Your table is all set. Enjoy yourselves!"

"We will!" Leslie assured him.

The waiter approached us and asked, "Can I get each of you something to drink?"

Pat, the organizer, spoke up. "I assume a little champagne is in order?"

That sounded like a good idea to the rest of us.

Pat did the honors, and the waiter left to fulfill her request.

"This has been a life-changing two days for me," Leslie acknowledged.

"My head is spinning with all that I've learned from every one of you. Thank you."

Here's to a wonderful life! A toast to health, to happiness… and to cash flow beyond our wildest dreams!

We each took turns and went around the table and shared what the past two days together meant to each of us and what we were going to do differently as a result.

Tracey finished with, "My life will never be the same. I knew before I got here that with all the changes at my company, as well as struggling financially to get ahead, that if I didn't change what I was doing that I was going to get exactly what I already had… or worse. For the first time in years I feel like I'm back in control of my life."

And at that moment our waiter appeared with Pat's choice and four champagne glasses, and he proceeded to pour the champagne.

"I have a toast!" Leslie announced.

We all raised our glasses.

"Congratulations to all of us. The support and encouragement from each of us amazes me. It's clear that we all want each of us to achieve the financial goals we set for ourselves. And I feel if I don't achieve my goals, then I am personally letting each of you down. That alone motivates me to keep going. I am so grateful to be a part of this group. To us!"

"To us!" we all chimed.

"To us… and our financial independence!" Tracey added.

We toasted again.

A Change In Thinking

Pat spoke up. "I woke up this morning thinking about our fateful lunch together in Honolulu 20 years ago. We were all somewhat like-minded, pursuing our career goals. It's fascinating to see the different directions we have all taken since then. But now here we are 20 years later and, instead of eagerly going after our career goals, we're again each on similar like-minded paths, yet this time pursuing our investment goals."

"And that is such a change for me," Leslie responded. "To realize that I, an artist since I could hold a crayon, spent two full days studying and talking about money, investing, and putting my own plan together to become financially independent simply amazes me. I'd have never dreamed of taking on something like this. I always thought finance and investing were way over my head, but I realize now that I can do this… and I'm excited about it!"

Tracey joined in. "I never recognized that the fear I felt about my husband losing his job or me getting laid-off was because I allowed others to control my life. I was waiting for my boss to tell me what my next 10 years would be. I'm going home with no fear toward that at all. I'm kicking myself that I didn't see that earlier, but better late than never. What I'm chuckling to myself about is that I hope I do get let go because then I'm sure there will be some sort of severance that I can put toward my new business. Now that's a change in thinking!"

"You nailed it on the head, Tracey," I replied. "It's all about a change in thinking. Changing the way you think. You don't look at your job or your paycheck as your life support any more, do you?"

"Not at all," she answered. "I've lived all my life thinking that there was only one way to make money, and that was through a paycheck. And I could only make as much as someone was willing to pay me, which is a limited amount. Now my mind has shifted to thinking the amount of money I can make is unlimited. I will determine how much money I make, both through my business and my investments. It truly is unlimited. That thought alone has made these past two days priceless."

Leslie said, "Until we started all these conversations I figured the only way I would make more money was to work additional jobs. I thought the paycheck was king also. I'd get exhausted just thinking about taking on a second or third job. Now I look at my current job as simply a tool to assist me in accomplishing my real goal of becoming financially free. I'll approach my work at the art gallery from a completely different point of view. I'll approach a number of things from a new viewpoint because so much of my time was spent worrying about paying my bills and being able to do the things I want to do. For the first time I can see the light at the end of the tunnel. I don't have to worry about it anymore. I just have to go do it!"

Change Starts With Me

"It's funny how things around you change when you change," I commented.

"That's so true," Leslie agreed. "I look at my job differently. I see my boss differently. I even look at my bills differently. But my job, my boss, and my bills haven't changed at all. I changed! I wonder if I'll look at my ex-husband differently. Miracles can happen."

Pat laughed. "I know what you mean. I came here hoping my husband would change, but it's not him who has to change, it's me. I've gone from thinking I can't do this without him to knowing I have to be the one to take those first steps. My intention is still that he will eventually join me, but it's up to me to make this happen. It's like a huge weight off my shoulders."

I added, "Who knows, you may even find some surprising changes in him when you return because of your shift in mindset."

Pat smiled at the thought.

"Since I seem to be the organizer of the group," Pat pointed out. "I have a proposal. We talked about keeping the momentum going from these two days. I think that is so important."

"I bet you're going to suggest what I've been thinking," Leslie said.

"I propose that for the next six months we have a one-hour conference call, once a month, with the four of us," Pat recommended. "Since Tracey, Leslie and I are just beginning, I know it would be really helpful to us. And if Kim would be willing to offer her input, then I think we'd have some great discussions as well as greater success. What do you all think?"

All four of us agreed. Pat made sure, on the spot, that we chose a day and time for the first call.

Just then the waiter appeared. "The owner noticed the four of you were obviously celebrating something very important this evening so she has sent over four glasses of champagne with her compliments. She says, 'Congratulations.'"

We happily thanked the waiter and the owner.

This time Tracey stood and announced, "A toast. Thanks to all of you, for the first time in a long time I feel that I am in control of my life. Here's to a wonderful life for us all – to health, to happiness… and to cash flow beyond our wildest dreams!

"Cheers!"

The End

P.S. Back at my house Pat checked her cell phone messages. There was a voicemail message from Janice. She exclaimed, "What was I thinking!? Was I crazy? That guy wasn't looking for a relationship he was looking for a free ride! What a loser! I can't believe I didn't see it. He wasn't even that good looking! I bet you all had a great couple of days together. Wish I had been there. What I'm really mad at myself about is that I wasted my time with this guy thinking he was my future when I could have been with the four of you creating my future."

A Final Thought

Many people say that money is not the most important thing in life. That may be true. However, money does affect everything that is important – your health, your education, and your quality of life.

Ultimately, money buys you one of two things: It buys you slavery or it buys you freedom. Slavery to your job, your debt, and sometimes even slavery within your relationships. Or it buys you freedom to live your life as you choose.

By making money important in my life, I bought my freedom. That's important to me… simply because I hate being told what to do.

Thank you for reading this book.

GENERAL FINANCE AND INVESTING TERMS

Accountant Has a formal accounting education, where a bookkeeper may not. An accountant will handle your day-to-day financial needs including the preparation of your financial statements. Accountants can also prepare tax returns.

Asset Something that puts money in your pocket whether you work or not. Assets include real estate, businesses, and paper assets such as stocks, bonds, and mutual funds.

Bonds May be tax-free Municipal Bonds, U.S. Government issued Treasuries, or Corporate Bonds which reflect debt by the issuing authority in exchange for interest payment to the purchaser.

Bookkeeper Keeps track of your bookkeeping records. In most cases you'll want a "full charge" bookkeeper – one who can pay bills, properly code them, track accounts receivable and payable, do payroll and prepare financial statements. Some bookkeepers will organize the information for an accountant who then prepares the financial statements and tax returns.

Cash Savings account, money market funds, certificates of deposit

Cash Flow The difference between the money flowing into your pocket as income and the money flowing out as expenses and debt. Cash flow may be either positive or negative.

Cash-On-Cash Return The bottom line on any investment – how much you'll make (or lose) for the amount of cash you've invested

Capital Gain The difference between the price at which you bought an investment and the price at which you sold it, less improvements made and other money invested in the investment.

Commodities Resources which include gold, silver, copper and other precious metals or food products such as pork bellies, wheat, corn, etc.

Common Stocks Equity issued by a company that gives the buyer ownership in the company. Stocks may or may not pay the buyer a dividend.

CPA (certified public accountant) Has passed a state exam, which gives them the CPA designation. There are many types of CPAs and specialties. Not all CPAs are tax specialists. CPAs may help you with management issues in your company (as a comptroller or chief financial officer), audit your financial statements for loan purposes (auditor), or help you with tax planning. (Known as a Chartered Accountant in other countries)

Earned Income Income that you work for.

Financial Statement There are several types of financial statements. An income statement shows a detailed account of income and expenses for a fixed period of time. A balance sheet includes the assets and liabilities at a particular time. A statement of cash flow details cash coming in and cash going out. Individuals, properties, and businesses all have their own financial statements.

Intellectual Property An original creative work, such as an invention, a product or a company brand, that is tangible and can be protected by a patent, trademark or copyright.

Leverage Doing more with less.

Liability Something that takes money out of your pocket. Liabilities include items such as credit card debt, mortgages, car loans, school loans, etc.

Passive Income Income you receive from businesses you invest in, royalties and rental real estate investments. It is income you are not working for.

Portfolio Income Income derived from paper assets such as stocks, bonds, mutual funds, etc.

Return on Investment (ROI) The amount of income you receive from an investment divided by the total amount invested into the investment.

Wealth As defined by R. Buckminster Fuller, the number of days you can survive without working for money, while still maintaining your same standard of living.

REAL ESTATE TERMS

Adjustable Rate Mortgage A mortgage loan whose interest rate changes periodically over the period of the loan.

Amortization Gradual repayment of a debt by periodic installments that cover both the principal and interest.

Annual Percentage Rate (APR) The effective rate of interest for a loan. The APR reflects all the costs of financing – including points, origination fees, and other finance charges – and is usually higher than the interest rate alone.

Appraisal An estimate or opinion of the value of a property by an impartial person skilled in the analysis and valuation of real estate.

Assumable Loan An existing loan on a property that the seller is able to pass on to the borrower.

Balloon Loan Mortgage loan in which the remaining amount is fully due and payable at a specified, predetermined date. Balloon loans may have a better interest rate, but you'll have to be prepared to pay the remaining balance of the loan in full (or obtain a new loan) at the specified time.

Cap The limit, expressed as a percentage, on the amount of an increase charged by a lender under the terms of an adjustable rate mortgage. Caps protect the borrower from large, unexpected interest rate increases.

CAP (capitalization)Rate This is the Net Operating Income divided by the purchase price. It does not take debt into account. It is an indicator of the value of the property. A general rule of thumb is the higher the CAP rate the lower the price of the property relative to its value. The lower the CAP rate the higher the price relative to its value.

Cash on Cash Return In real estate, it's a percentage figure determined by dividing the annual cash flow of a property by the amount of cash put into the property (typically the down payment and closing costs.)

Closing The process by which ownership of a property passes from the seller to the buyer. Closing includes the delivery of a deed, financial adjustments, the signing of notes, and the disbursement of funds necessary to complete the sale.

Closing Agent A third-party agent of your choosing (an attorney, escrow agent, representative of the title company, or a professional closing agent),who handles all aspects of the actual transaction.

Closing Costs The expenses incurred in the completion of a real estate transaction.

Contingency A condition in an offer sheet or contract that must be met before the deal can go forward.

Cost Segregation An accounting strategy which allows you to depreciate your property at an accelerated rate.

Counter Offer A response to an offer to purchase a property that introduces new or different terms and conditions.

Credit Report An assessment, provided by a local retail credit association, of an individual's ability to repay debt.

Debt The mortgage or loan on a property

Deferred Maintenance Necessary repairs and upkeep that have been left undone by the seller. Maintenance that has been deferred can represent an opportunity in a deal, allowing you to negotiate a lower price.

Down Payment Cash paid by the buyer at closing, representing a percentage of the purchase price. Different types of loans may require different percentages of down payment.

Due Diligence A research process that provides accurate and complete information regarding the physical, financial, and legal attributes of a property.

Equity The value of a real estate property less the mortgage and other liabilities related to it.

Escrow Money or property put into the custody of a 3rd party until certain conditions are met.

Estoppel Certificate A written statement by each tenant outlining the amount of rent being paid and whether any concessions have been promised to the tenant during the rest of the term of the lease.

Eviction The process of legally removing a tenant from a rental unit or rental property. Evictions are granted for non-payment of rent or other breach with the terms of the lease.

Financing Terms This specifies the type of loan (new, seller financing, assumable, etc.) available, the amount to be financed, as well as an estimated interest rate.

Fixed Rate Mortgage A mortgage loan whose interest rate is fixed for a portion of or the entire term of the loan. The interest rate will usually be higher than that of an adjustable rate mortgage.

Fixer-Upper A property that needs repairs and renovation.

Foreclosure A legal process whereby a mortgage is terminated and possession of the property is taken over by the lender. Foreclosures usually occur for failure to make payments.

FSBO For Sale by Owner – a property being sold without contracting a real estate professional's services.

Internal Rate of Return (IRR) This is a return on investment that assumes all the income (passive/cash flow) you receive is immediately reinvested so that you would be getting a return on that money as well.

Interest The amount, expressed as a percentage of the total, that a lender charges a borrower for a loan.

Lease A legally binding, contractual agreement between landlord and tenant for the occupancy of a rental property. A strong lease stipulates all terms and conditions of the landlord-tenant relationship.

Leverage In real estate, borrowing money from a financial lender to purchase a property is a form of leverage. You put down a small percentage of money, the bank loans you the rest, and you purchase 100% of the property.

Loan Servicing The paperwork involved in handling mortgage loans.

Loan-to-Value Ratio The amount of a mortgage loan compared to the value of the property purchased. A $100,000 house with a loan of $80,000 has an 80% loan-to-value ratio.

Maturity The date when a loan is due in full.

Mortgage A written agreement that gives the lender an interest in the property as security for a loan.

Mortgage Brokers Professionals who match financial institutions with money to lend to investors who want to borrow.

Notice A period of time, stipulated in writing, before a stated action will take place. Leases usually specify the amount of notice the landlord must give the tenant before inspecting the property, charging late fees, or beginning the eviction process.

Offer Sheet Also known as a letter of intent, a proposal to enter into an agreement to purchase a specific property from another party.

Origination Fees Charges to a borrower, stated as a percentage of the loan amount, for costs and fees associated with issuing the loan.

PITI Abbreviation for principal, interest, taxes, and insurance. The acronym is used to describe what may be included in the monthly repayment of a mortgage loan.

Point One percent of a mortgage loan amount. A point is an additional charge by the lender at the time of loan origination as a placement or service fee.

Prepayment Penalty A fee charged to the borrower if the mortgage loan is paid off before its full term.

Private Mortgage Insurance (PMI)
Insurance against default issued by a private company on conventional mortgage loans. Such insurance is usually required when the down payment is less than 20%.

Pro Forma A projected financial statement showing income, expenses, and financing terms typically based on anticipated, not actual, numbers.

Real Estate Land and buildings.

Real Estate Purchase Contract Also known as an agreement of sale, a legally binding agreement between buyer and seller stipulating the terms and conditions of the sale of a real estate property.

Seller Financing The seller acts as the bank and finances any portion of the purchase price for the buyer. The buyer pays the seller the principal and interest agreed upon.

Service Contract A written agreement for a maintenance provider – such as a landscaper, plumber, electrician, or handyman – to perform routine maintenance repairs, and/or emergency service. Service contracts are worthwhile if you own several properties and have frequent service requests.

Term The period of time until a loan must be repaid.

Title Deed A legal document showing ownership to a specific property.

Underwriting The formal approval or denial of a loan based on the purchaser's ability to pay off the loan and the value of the property as collateral.

Vacancy Rate A figure representing either the percentage of units unrented or the percentage of time a single unit remains unrented during the year.

Zoning Laws Regulations governing land use, population density, an building size and use. Set by local governments, zoning laws typically change as communities develop.

Glossary of Terms for Analyzing Investment Properties

Price Per Unit The asking or purchase price of a property divided by the total number of rental units

Price Per Square Foot The asking or purchase price divided by the total rentable square footage.

Unit Mix The type of units of a property – i.e. studio, 1 bedroom/1 bath, 2 bedroom/1 bath – and the quantity of each type of unit.

Rent Per Square Foot Divide the rent of a unit by the total number of square feet of that unit. The rent per square foot gives you a more accurate picture when comparing rents of similar properties.

Gross Income Stated as monthly and/or annually, this is the total of all income from all units whether they are actually rented or not.

Vacancy Rate This is the percentage of rent not collect based upon unrented units. If your gross income is $1000 and your vacancy rate is 10% then you will collect $1000 – $100 or $900 in income.

Other Income This is additional income collected in the form of laundry, parking, vending machines, etc.

Loss to Lease This occurs when you are charging rents below what the market in charging. To calculate subtract the actual rents you are receiving from the market rent.

Operating Expenses This includes all the expenses attributed to the operation of the property.

Net Operating Income The total collected income less the total operating expenses.

Debt or Debt Service The debt or mortgage payment on a property.

Cash Flow The profit or loss on an investment property. The calculation for cash flow is total collected income, less the operating expenses, less the debt service equals your cash flow.

Cash on Cash Return on Investment This is the amount of annual cash flow divided by the amount of cash you have put into the deal (primarily the down payment). It is shown as a percentage.

Paper Asset Terms

Amex (American Stock Exchange) The rival New York Curb Exchange was founded in 1842. Its name said it all: trading actually took place on the street until it moved indoors in 1921. In 1953, the Curb Exchange became the American Stock Exchange.

Blue Chip Stocks Is a term borrowed from poker, where the blue chips are the most valuable, and refers to the stocks of the largest, most consistently profitable corporations. The list isn't official – and it does change.

Book Value Is the difference between the company's assets and liabilities. A small or low book value from too much debt, for example, means that the company's profits will be limited even if it does lots of business. Sometimes a low book value means that assets are underes-timated; experts consider these companies a good companies.

Call Options

> **Buy** – The right to buy the underlying item at the strike price until the expiration date.

> **Sell** – Selling the right to buy the underlying item from you at the strike price until the expiration date. Known as writing a call.

Commodities Commodities are raw materials: the wheat in bread, the silver in earrings, the oil in gasoline, and a thousand other products. Commodity prices are based on supply and demand.

Common Stock Ownership shares in a corporation. They are sold initially by the corporation and then traded among investors. Investors who buy them expect to earn dividends as their part of the profits, and hope that the price of the stock will go up so their investment will be worth more. Common stocks offer no performance guarantees, but over time have produced a better return than other investments.

Derivative A contact whose value is based on the performance of an underlying financial asset, index, or other investment.

Dividend Distribution of earnings to shareholders, prorated by class of security and paid in the form of money, stock, script, or, rarely, company products or property.

Dividend Yield Annual percentage of return earned by an investor on a common or preferred stock. The yield is determined by dividing the amount of annual dividends per share, called the indicated dividend, by the current market price per share of the stock.

DJIA (Dow Jones Industrial Average) An index which measures the market performance of it's 30 component stocks over time.

Earnings Per Share Are calculated by dividing the number of shares into the profit. If earnings increase each year, the company is growing.

Equities Ownership interest possessed by shareholders in a corporation-stock as opposed to bonds.

Futures Are obligations to buy or sell a specific commodity-such as corn or gold-on a specific day for a preset price.

Hedge Fund Private investment partnership (for U.S. investors) or an offshore investment corporation (for non U.S. or tax exempt investors) in which the general partner has made a substantial personal investment, and whose offering memorandum allows for the fund to take both long and short positions, use leverage and derivatives, and invest in many markets.

IPO (Initial Public Offering) Taking a company public, which means making it possible for investors to buy the stock, the management makes an initial public offering (IPO).

Municipal Bonds The not-so-secret charm of municipal bonds is their tax exempt status. Investors don't have to share their earnings with the IRS-or state taxing authorities.

Mutual Funds Professionally managed portfolio of Stocks or Bonds.

Nasdaq (National Association of Securities Dealers) The principal home of top U.S. growth companies as well as International companies trading shares in the U.S. Nasdaq real-time quotes are transmitted through an International computer and telecommunications network to more than 1.3 million users in 83 countries.

NYSE (New York Stock Exchange) The New York Stock Exchange provides the facilities for stock trading and rules under which trading takes place. It has no responsibility for setting the price of a stock. That is the result of supply and demand, and the trading process.

OTC (Over The Counter) Stocks in more than 28,000 small and new companies are traded in the over-the-counter market. The term originated at the time when you actually bought stock over the counter from a local broker.

Preferred Stock Are also ownership shares issued by a corporation and traded by investors. They are sold initially by the corporation and then traded among investors.

Propsectus Formal written offer to sell securities that set forth the plan for a proposed business enterprise or facts concerning an existing one that an investor needs to make an informed decision.

Put Option

> **Buy** – The right to sell the underlying item at the strike price until the expiration date.

> **Sell** – Selling the right to sell the underlying item to you until the expiration date. Known as writing a put.

Return On Equity Is a percentage figured by dividing a company's earnings per share by its book value.

Reverse Split In a reverse split you exchange more stocks for fewer-say ten for five-and the price increases accordingly. Reverse splits are sometimes used to raise a stocks price.

SEC In the wake of the great depression and the stock trading scandals that it exposed, the U.S. government created Securities and Exchange Commission (SEC) in 1934. Its mission is to regulate the activities of stock traders.

Selling Short Sale of a security or commodity futures contract that is not owned by the seller; a technique used (1) to take advantage of an anticipated decline in the price or (2) to protect a profit in a long position.

Stockbroker Employee of a stock exchange member broker/dealer who acts as an Account Executive for clients.

Stock Split More shares created at lower price per share. Stockholders profit if price goes back up.

Types of bonds

Corporate Bonds – Are readily available to investors as companies use them rather than bank loans to finance expansion and other activities.

Municipal Bonds – More than 1 million municipal bonds are issued by states, cities and other local governments to pay for construction and other projects.

T-Bonds And T-Notes – These are long-term debt issues of the Federal government funding to keep operations running and to pay interest on national debt.

T-Bills – Treasury bills are the largest component of the money market – the market for short-term debt securities. The government uses them to raise money for immediate spending at lower rates than bonds or notes.

Agency Bonds – The most popular and well-known are the bonds of mortgage association, nicknamed Ginnie Mae, Fannie Mae, and Freddie Mac. But many federal and state agencies also issue bonds to raise money for their operations and projects.

U.S. Treasury Bonds The U.S. Treasury offers three choices: bonds, bills, and notes. A key difference is their term, from 13 weeks to 30 years.

Venture Capital Important source for financing for start-up companies or others embarking on new turnaround ventures that entail some investment risk but offer the potential for above-average future profits; also called risk capital.

KIM KIYOSAKI

Kim is a perfect example of a woman who knew absolutely nothing about money or the world of investing. She knew early on that she would not follow a conventional way of life, simply because she was fiercely independent, competitive, and had a real problem being told what to do.

Her business career began in advertising, and her entrepreneurial spirit emerged shortly thereafter. She launched her first business venture in 1984. Since then she and her husband, Robert, have built several successful companies, the latest, along with partner Sharon Lechter, being The Rich Dad Company best known for the best-selling book *Rich Dad Poor Dad*.

Kim began her investing career in 1989. After her first investment she soon realized that investing would be her road to freedom, and she pursued it fervently. Today she controls millions of dollars of investment property as well as other investment assets.

A businesswoman and investor, Kim is passionate about teaching women the importance of investing and taking control of their financial futures.

Bestselling Books by
Robert T. Kiyosaki & Sharon L. Lechter

Rich Dad Poor Dad
What the Rich Teach Their Kids About Money
that the Poor and Middle Class Do Not

Rich Dad's CASHFLOW Quadrant
Rich Dad's Guide to Financial Freedom

Rich Dad's Guide to Investing
What the Rich Invest In that the Poor and Middle Class Do Not

Rich Dad's Rich Kid Smart Kid
Give Your Child a Financial Head Start

Rich Dad's Retire Young Retire Rich
How to Get Rich Quickly and Stay Rich Forever

Rich Dad's Prophecy
Why the Biggest Stock Market Crash in History is Still Coming...
And How You Can Prepare Yourself and Profit From it!

Rich Dad's Success Stories
Real-Life Success Stories from Real-Life People
Who Followed the Rich Dad Lessons

Rich Dad's Guide to Becoming Rich Without Cutting Up Your Credit Cards
Turn "Bad Debt" into "Good Debt"

Rich Dad's Who Took My Money?
Why Slow Investors Lose and Fast Money Wins!

Rich Dad Poor Dad for Teens
The Secrets About Money – That You Don't Learn In School!

Rich Dad's Escape from the Rat Race
How to Become a Rich Kid by Following Rich Dad's Advice

Rich Dad's Before You Quit Your Job
Ten Real-Life Lessons Every Entrepreneur Should Know
About Building a Multi-Million Dollar Business

Rich Dad's Teach TO BE *Rich*

- Why did a *USA Today* survey find that the greatest fear of Americans is running out of money in retirement?

- Why is money, as a subject, not taught in school?

- Why is the average American the biggest debtor in the world?

This is a great program to use with your women's investment study group!

Rich Dad's Teach To Be Rich will provide answers to these questions and more. It will explain the problem, but more importantly, define the solution …and the solution is to become rich… by teaching others to be rich.

More than a book on teaching, *Rich Dad's Teach To Be Rich* is about Robert's quest to find out how we learn and why so many people do not like school… even though they want to learn.

$ **99**

This set includes a Book, Workbook, and 3 DVDs

For more information:
visit www.richdad.com

"This book took away all the fear I had with respect to $$
and investing. The best $20 I've ever spent!"

Betty • Pescadero, California

"*Rich Woman* is my good luck charm to be rich!"

Lorraine • Suisun City, Ca

"From reading *Rich Woman*, I feel inspired to stop messing
around and get my financial future taken care of!"

Jane • Phoenix, Arizona

"*Rich Woman* is a very important book for women of all ages.
It teaches us to take responsibility for our finances, and
delivers a great overview of where and how to get started."

Dawn • San Jose, California

| To contact Rich Woman | visit www.richwoman.com
or call 1-800-308-3585 |
| To order Rich Woman books | visit www.richwoman.com |

| To contact Rich Dad | visit www.richdad.com
or call 1-800-308-3585 |
| To order Rich Dad books | visit www.twbookmark.com |

For more information:

The Rich Dad Company

4330 N. Civic Center Plaza, Suite 100 Scottsdale, Arizona 85251

TEL: (800) 308-3585 • Fax: (480) 348-1349 • E-mail: service@richdad.com